A Picture of Faith

A Picture of Faith

A meditation on the imagery
of Christ in Glory

Michael Sadgrove

First published in 1995 by
KEVIN MAYHEW LTD
Rattlesden
Bury St Edmunds
Suffolk IP30 0SZ

© 1995 Michael Sadgrove

ISBN   0 86209 526 3
Catalogue No 1500008

Front cover: The Crucifixion panel from *Christ in Glory in the
Tetramorph* by Graham Sutherland (1903-1980).
Photograph courtesy of Jason Tilley.

Cover design by Graham Johnstone
Typesetting and Page Creation by Anne Haskell
in Simoncini Garamond (Monotype)
Printed in Hong Kong

PREFACE

THIS BOOK is the product of mid-life. For me, as for many people, it has been a time to look again at life, reassess meanings and goals, explore the significance of the past and find new direction for the future. Above all, it has been a time of rediscovering what ultimately *matters* in life and where God belongs in the story.

During these key years of thought and reflection, I have had the good fortune to work at Coventry Cathedral. In that time, I have been fascinated by Graham Sutherland's tapestry of Christ in Glory that dominates the nave. I have experienced it in many different lights: in summer and winter, by day and by night, at worship and in prayer, from below and from above. Often, I have come into the Cathedral for nothing else but the sheer pleasure of seeing it again. Like the sky or the sea, it is never the same two days running.

I have found the tapestry becoming more and more a focus for my own developing self-understanding as a human being and as a Christian. Any work of art, I imagine, or piece of literature, or landscape, or experience of pain or pleasure, might have provided such a focus. I can only say that for me, the tapestry was in the right place at the right time. It has been a kind of gift, though only time will tell whether the insights I have wrestled with at its feet have been grasped and learned well enough to last.

This book is a meditation on this (to me) great work of art. It is not a book *about* the tapestry or its artist. That is work for art critics and historians, and I would not want to encroach on their territory, though I suppose I do trespass into the domain of interpretation from time to time. What I have tried to offer is a meditation on the tapestry's symbols – its powerful, often shifting, imagery that seems to me to have so much to say about the human condition, about our ultimate concerns, about our faith in God.

I write, therefore, as a human being endeavouring to make sense out of life, and hoping, if I can, to help others who want to do the same. The tapestry, as I say early on in the book, makes of us explorers of the spirit. I offer these reflections as one explorer to others, in the hope that we may, perhaps, travel part of the way together. I should like to think of what I have written as a modest piece of prayed theology illuminated by the insights of poets and painters, writers, musicians and spiritual guides down the ages.

Much of this book was written during a period of sabbatical leave in 1991, and I would like to thank the Provost and my other colleagues at the Cathedral for generously allowing me that time of study and reflection. I owe a particular debt of thanks to Heather Wallace for goading me into finishing the book, and to Mary Burton for typing the first draft. Amongst those who have offered encouragement, help and criticism, I am especially grateful to Joan Browne, Tony Bryer; and Jo Donlevy of Kevin Mayhew. Kundry, the family cat, kept me company during much of the writing, when the house was empty and I would otherwise have been quite alone. But it is to my family that I owe the greatest debt of all, especially to my wife, for helping me, so often, to see both the tapestry and human life in new and richer ways. To her I dedicate this book with love and gratitude.

MICHAEL SADGROVE
COVENTRY, LENT 1994

CONTENTS

Part 1: Approaching

Part 2: Closer In

Part 3: Moving Out Again

ILLUSTRATIONS

For Jenny

Part One

APPROACHING

'What are you smiling at?' . . . I had not realised
I was smiling. 'At the tapestry,' I said. 'It is so
happy.' 'Yes . . . our art is happy.'

Andrew Harvey, *A Journey in Ladakh*

1

From Far Off

I CAN CLEARLY remember the first time I ever saw mountains. I was a boy of seven, brought up in suburban London. The nearest thing to a hill was Muswell Hill where we lived, and on whose flank the brakes of my pavement cycle had once failed, precipitating me more ignominiously than painfully into a tree that providence had placed in my path. That summer, we holidayed in South Wales. As we approached the Welsh border, suddenly round a bend in the road, I could see a great wall of mountains in the distance, a rampart, high and mysterious, far off, and wreathed in clouds. I suppose they were the Black Mountains, which many years later I learned to love as a walker.

I am reminded of that sight of distant splendour as I approach the Great Tapestry of Coventry Cathedral, which is the subject of my book. Like mountains, I need to stand at a distance to begin with, take in what is before me. To get too close too soon would be to rush what must take time. Distances have their own perspective to offer, a necessary one if we are to see things as a whole, and not just in part.

So I stop at the west end of the long nave, and try to take in the far-off splendour of Graham Sutherland's tapestry, this mountain I am about to scale.

How It Came to Be

Amongst the main facts of the tapestry are these. In 1952, Sutherland accepted the invitation of Sir Basil Spence, the architect who had won the competition to design the new Coventry Cathedral, to create the tapestry. The design process, which included three maquettes or cartoons in oils, and innumerable detailed studies, occupied the years from that date until 1958.[1] After various trials, the weaving was begun in 1959 by the Pinton Frères at Felletin near Aubusson, a centre of tapestry-making since the middle ages. The tapestry was made as a single piece, the twelve weavers working from full-sized photographic enlargements of the final cartoon. This work took two and a half years. The tapestry arrived in the Cathedral in March 1962, in time for the consecration on 25 May. It measures 74 feet 8 inches by 38 feet, and weighs just over one ton. At the time, it was the largest tapestry in the world. Around 900 dyes were used in its making, and the colours are said to be good for 500 years.[2]

I do not need to know any of this when I approach the tapestry, any more than I need to know the exact height of the mountains I see in the distance, or their geological history. But faced with a work of art on such an immense scale, I am bound to be curious. In one sense, my curiosity is irrelevant to the 'message' of the tapestry, and might even get in the way. I might miss the wood for the trees, just as some of the more recondite forms of biblical scholarship seem not to hear the word that speaks out of the words of the ancient scriptures. I need to be attentive to the tapestry, take in what is there, be open to what God might say to me through it.

Yet, at the same time, the story of its making does carry its own message, it seems to me, for the tapestry is the work of human hands, whose 'signature' appears on the work itself. Thus, the 'making' is part of the 'message', as I shall explore in the final chapter of this book. How it came to be is part of what it now is, just as how I came to be belongs to the story of who I am, and why. So although my meditation is about the *meaning* of the tapestry, rather than its making, I must not separate them too rigidly. Each will inform the other.

UPWARD AND INWARD

As I enter Coventry Cathedral then, I am at once grasped by what I see at the other end of the building. Where I expect there to be a window flooding the church with light, I find instead a wall. At first sight, especially on a dull day, that far end can look disconcertingly opaque: there is nothing to see *through* to. Transparency is important in places of worship, that sense that what goes on in them isn't confined to their walls but has something to do with the world outside, with the lives we ordinary human beings have to live.

Of course, Coventry *is* a transparent cathedral – more than many. The great glass screen through which we enter is its massive statement that worship and living belong together. You leave the cathedral at the end of worship, and are hardly conscious of having crossed any threshold as you go: the glass is as clear as air. You 'go in peace', and it is as if liturgy and life become one. That is as it should be.

But that is to anticipate the end of my meditation. Here, I am looking along the Cathedral, *upward*, or perhaps looking *inward*, if to turn round and gaze through the glass screen is to look outward. Upward and inward: those are the movements I begin to make as I approach the tapestry. And as I think about those two movements, I realise that they are the fundamental movements of faith, the movements every religious man or woman has to make if his or her faith is to be a living, life-changing experience.

The *upward* movement toward the tapestry is the way of transcendence. This is the movement *away* from myself, the movement towards what is beyond me, greater than me, or, as the theologians say, 'other'. For me, the tapestry is one of the great symbols of transcendence in the Cathedral. Christ in Glory: in one way, he is infinitely beyond my reach, not remote or far-off in a personal sense, for I know that he is grace and love. Yet precisely *because* he is grace and love beyond what I can even begin to conceive, I know I am in the presence of deep mystery. I am drawn out of myself, upward, towards glory, towards Christ in Glory, towards the vision of God himself. In an important sense, I begin to learn what the spiritual guides down the ages call self-forgetfulness, or detachment.

But, paradoxically, this upward movement is paralleled by an inward movement, a movement *toward* myself, *into* myself. This is the process of self-discovery or, if you like, the discovery that to move inwards is itself to move, not away from God but towards him. This is the way of immanence, the insight that God is as much within us as beyond us, as ready to be found at

the core of our being as he is infinitely beyond our compre-
hension or grasp. The oracle at Delphi pronounced: 'know
yourself', as if to say that to know myself is to know God; to find
myself is to find God. 'God is nearer to us than our own soul'
says Mother Julian of Norwich.[3] And to me, the tapestry draws
me on this all-important quest for inwardness. It draws me out
of myself, true. But at the same time, I find I am drawn to a
more inward experience of life too. To paraphrase a saying of
St Augustine, it is not only the mystery of God that I see on the
great tapestry, but also the mystery of myself.

THE VISION AND THE TASK

Moving upward, moving inward: all of religion is there, all of
life, for what more is there to life than this twofold task, which
is one task, of knowing God and knowing myself? I use the
word 'task', for I believe that it is 'work', God's work and ours.
It involves cost, struggle, even pain. The New Testament talks
about it as a kind of death: dying to myself, in order to live more
abundantly, losing in order to find. It is not easy to be a
Christian, to take up this cross. But I also want to believe that
religion is more than a task. I want to believe that it is an
adventure, the most exciting, exhilarating adventure a man or
woman can ever embark on. I want to discover what happiness
means as well as duty, what it means to enjoy God as well as
glorify him. I am ready for hardship, but I also look for
fulfilment, for meaning and for purpose in life.

I have an instinct that the Great Tapestry can help me in this
adventure and this task. I cannot know, of course, until I come
a little nearer, approach this monumental figure of Christ in
Glory, risk what I might need to lose in order to find. I know I
must draw near with faith.

I have always loved the paintings of Rembrandt. The
wisdom, the insight, the spirituality of this most humane of
painters are unmatched in the history of art. The marvel, to me,
is what Rembrandt achieves through the medium of paint. His
technique is to apply the paint very thickly; you might almost

say opaquely. And yet, no painting glows like a Rembrandt, or is more transparent to the lives and stories of the men and women who come to life, as I want to put it, not *in* his canvasses so much as *across* them. Again, there is this sense that there is a life depicted 'on the other side', a life that the artist's genius succeeds in communicating to us with a vividness undimmed with the passing of the centuries.[4]

As I stand at a distance, I begin to sense that the tapestry, too, is not as solid, as opaque, as it first seemed. The surface appears less flat, begins to acquire depth. The green looks as if it is illuminated from within, as it casts its glow across the entire nave. And above all, the face of Christ seems to come to life. It is as if someone is *there*, on the 'other side' of the tapestry, so to speak; a Presence who draws me, and holds me, and above all, *knows* me. There is a transparency here after all, an invitation to a new way of seeing that points the way upward and inward, the way to myself, the way to God.

'CHRIST IN GLORY IN THE TETRAMORPH'

This huge tapestry of an enthroned Christ in Glory surrounded by symbols of the four Evangelists was to carry the main burden of an emotional impact that was to dominate the building and establish a mood to which the whole of the interior was to be subordinated.[5]

This 'emotional impact' of the tapestry is, I think, what I am most conscious of as I stand at a distance and try to take it in. Even now that I know the tapestry fairly well, its ability to stop me in my tracks and arrest me still comes as a surprise. It is like having a partner or friend you thought you knew well, whose conversation you thought you could accurately predict, only to find that he or she still has the capacity to astonish, delight, perhaps disturb you in your self-assurance.

One of my favourite places for private prayer, paradoxically, is in the middle of the nave, the most public place in the whole

Cathedral. It is not (I hope) that I need or want to be *seen* praying – for I believe very much in the precept of the Sermon on the Mount that the only kind of prayer God is really interested in is what happens behind closed doors, 'in secret' as Jesus puts it.[6] The paradox is that this highly public, visible place actually *feels*, and probably is, as secret and anonymous as anywhere. I doubt whether I am paid very much attention as I sit alone amid the sea of chairs, any more than a solitary figure on a park bench in the middle of London commands more than a fleeting glance from those passing by.

What makes it attractive to me is the *feeling* of solitude here. There is a sense of exposure, a consciousness of being grasped by a vast space not unlike what I experience on the high fells or at sea. I wonder sometimes whether religion doesn't pay too much attention to recreating dark, womb-like experiences rather than enabling us to breathe in the cooler, clearer, if more astringent air of the wide open spaces.

This may be an argument for the existence of cathedrals. But I am very aware that the tapestry has much to do with what I experience as I sit silently in the nave and try to be open to truth and to God. It is that elusive quality I can only call presence that I am meaning. I identify it with two things on the tapestry. There is its restful, all-pervasive green that seems to want to flood into my being, with all that it promises of healing, renewal and growth. And there is the figure of Christ in glory, at once strong and gentle, noble yet tender, whose face tells of a 'love that will not let me go', whose glory is somehow *accessible*, within reach.

Then the other images on this extraordinary hanging begin to come into focus: the swirling energies of the four living creatures as they gyrate, it seems, around the still centre of Christ haloed at the heart of the tapestry; the 'high window' above him, through which pours light from some far-off place, with its Dove descending as if on a sunbeam; the human figure dwarfed between the feet of Christ, and below, the mysterious chalice with its serpent rising out of its depths; the archangel Michael wrestling with Satan; and underneath all this, barely hinted at from the nave, the crucifixion panel, ashen-hued, the tragic antipole to the glory above it.

THE DRAMA OF LOVE

I am tempted, sometimes, to think of the tapestry as if it were the backcloth to a drama enacted in front of it, like the backdrop of some theatrical set. It isn't a bad analogy: the sacred liturgy *is* a drama, the church *is* a theatre, and the tapestry *is* indisputably a reredos that not only gives setting and colour to the liturgy, but in an important sense, presides over it. The liturgy, after all, belongs not to us, but to Christ in Glory.

But as I ponder it and feel myself pulled into its life a little more, I realise that the drama is taking place *within* the tapestry itself. I mean, of course, the everlasting drama of God's love moving out towards the whole creation, redeeming it, reconciling it to himself. Both the tragedy and the comedy of the divine drama are there. The tragedy recognises the reality of evil and the divine struggle with it epitomised by St Michael and the devil, and by the agonised crucifixion scene below. The comedy celebrates the triumph of love, the dance of creation around the figure of Christ, the light and glory flooding into the tapestry from beyond, transfiguring it with laughter and joy.

And because I know both tragedy and comedy in my own life, I find the tapestry resonates with my own experience. Its drama is my drama, for what God is wanting to do with his creation is what he is wanting to do in my own life too, and in the life of human society. I am the stage where all this is acted out, day by day, hour by hour, where God's love makes some breakthrough, claims some new ground; or else is forced back again by some new refusal, yet another 'no' to grace and truth.

All this is why, for me, the tapestry 'works': because I recognise there the issues that are daily confronting my own life and the life of the world. Like true theatre, there is no escaping life's realities; rather, there is a new engagement with them through what has been focused and acted out for us on stage. Just as theatre changes things, so I want to believe that the tapestry can change things – at the very least, my own attitudes and priorities, what I believe about God, the world and myself.

And that, I trust, is where my exploration of the tapestry may be leading me. Like the mountains that so impressed me as a child, there is something about the tapestry's *largeness* that entices me. 'Largeness' is the word Sutherland uses to describe the work of the great artists who inspired him: Picasso, Goya, Rembrandt. 'Deeply rooted in them is a genius for expression, a largeness of spirit, great perspicacity and curiosity.'[7] Perhaps the tapestry may inspire those same qualities in me, too, as I draw nearer to it: a 'largeness of spirit' that will enable me to become more giving, more generous towards God and my neighbour; a 'perspicacity' that will lead me to be more discerning, more discriminating in the choices I make; a 'curiosity' that will prevent me from ever thinking I have plumbed the mystery of living, the mystery of God.

And finally, I dare to ask, if not for a 'genius for expression', then at least for some little confidence in sharing God's gift with others, becoming, in a small way, a channel for his light, his life and his love.

2

A MAGIC CARPET

A LIFE-SPEAKING STORY

STORIES have always been important to me. I still return with pleasure and deepening appreciation to the story books I have had with me since childhood. A favourite story is the 'Prince and the Fairy', one of the *Arabian Nights*, those marvellous tales told by an oriental princess, Sheherezade, to save herself from execution. There is something very profound in the thought that telling stories is connected with salvation. One modern fiction writer calls story-telling 'life-speaking.'[1] When we tell the gospel story, the good news, we know it is 'life-speaking' in its deepest sense. Like the *Arabian Nights* that saved Sheherezade from death, our story is the story that saves us, sustains us and keeps us alive from one day to the next.

The particular story I have in mind has the age-old theme of royal marriage. The Sultan's three sons all wish to marry a certain princess. So he sets them all a challenge. They must return in a year's time with the most wonderful gift they can find, 'something strange curious and enchanted' he enjoins. Whoever wins the contest wins the bride. So one brother comes up with a magic looking-glass through which he can see whatever he wishes. The second produces a magic apple that can cure any disease. It would not be difficult to theologise at length on both these gifts, to see in them symbols of self-knowledge and healing brought by the knowledge of God.

But it is the third son, Husain, whose offering has passed into our own folklore. It is a magic carpet that will carry a person anywhere in the world. All that is required is to take the risk of stepping on to the carpet and resolve to travel. And here, tradition embellishes the tale in one of two ways. Some say that you had to express a wish for a chosen destination: knowing where you wanted to go, the carpet would take you there. Others say that the carpet had a mind of its own: your journey would be a surprise, a mystery tour. You couldn't ever quite predict what the carpet would do with you next.

As a child, I would dream for hours about this magic carpet that could bear people up, lift them above the clouds, transport them to new realms. I would act out the fantasy by jumping on and off the living-room carpet (conveniently, a highly patterned, coloured, Persian carpet that lent verisimilitude to my oriental daydreams.) And this fantasy continues to carry meaning for me when I meditate on the tapestry. Here is a carpet that makes journeys possible: not ordinary journeys, but extraordinary ones that break new horizons and defy the imagination. With this carpet, you are always on the move to somewhere new. You never stand still.

GOD OF SURPRISES[2]

Both these ways of telling the tale of Husain's magic carpet have something to say to me. It seems to me that it is true of most travel that I *both* have an idea where I am going, *and* am surprised in some way when I get there. In other words, I very rarely set out on a complete mystery tour. I have a goal in mind, or at least a general sense that I am heading in this direction rather than that. And yet I think it is fair to say that no journey will ever be entirely as I predict it. There will be some new experience on the way; something different to notice on arrival; something that has gone on inside me that is the result simply of packing a bag, leaving the well-known and the secure environment of home, and opening myself up to what is at least *slightly* strange and unfamiliar and new.

I find that every life-journey I make is full of surprises: marriage, for instance, or my choice of career or how I am going to spend my leisure time. But even the commonest 'journeys' have, or ought to have, the capacity to take me by surprise, pull me up short, make me think. Take church going, for instance. For many of us, nothing could be more familiar than this weekly journey we make to worship God on a Sunday morning. Very probably I have my own routine. I expect to arrive five minutes before the service begins, to sit in my own familiar seat next to people I know, enter into a liturgy I am familiar with and sing hymns I have known since childhood. The sermon will last for twelve minutes, and if the service is running to time, I shall stay for coffee and discussion afterwards before setting off home to put the finishing touches to the Sunday lunch.

Now, as a liturgist I want to say that this is very important. I need this kind of security the liturgy offers, what I call its *mothering* aspect. Only then will I be relaxed and open enough to God for him to speak to me. But that is precisely the point at which things become *unpredictable*. For as soon as God begins to address me through the liturgy, to confront, challenge, invite me in a new way, the journey has become a surprise. I will not, and can never, leave worship the same as I came in, not if I have truly met God there and taken him into myself in word and sacrament. There has been transformation and change. And again, as a liturgist I need to remember that worship, if it does not change us for the better or offer us a profounder vision to live by, is no more than a religious performance. So although, in one sense, I know where the journey of worship is taking me Sunday by Sunday, in another sense, it will always be a divine surprise.

And if God is a God of the everyday, then all of life should be like this.

CROSSING OVER

So I begin to see how the tapestry beckons me on a journey that changes me. It summons me to be an explorer, a Magellan or Columbus of the human spirit. As I look at the great figure of Christ in glory, I feel that everything is under review: my own life, the life of the world, prayer, politics, priorities. I must learn to look at everything in a new way, all over again, as if *sub specie aeternitatis*, under the searching, loving, judging gaze of Christ. Nothing can remain untouched, unaffected. I must pack my bags, travel as light as I can of what would hold me back and become a pilgrim, embarking on a journey of exploration that

I know will be as much a journey towards the world, towards other people, as it will be a journey into God.

The idea of the journey is a basic metaphor of life. In the imagery of the Bible, the exodus journey from slavery to freedom, the long march through sea and desert to a land of promise, has become a picture, for whole nations no less than individuals, of what is glimpsed as life's God-given process, a constant movement forwards into a deeper, more life-giving, more wholesome way of living. Spiritual writings like Dante's *Divine Comedy* and Bunyan's *Pilgrim's Progress* have inspired generations of religious people to understand their lives as a pilgrimage towards a God-given destiny. So to see in the tale of Husain's magic carpet a powerful image of the spiritual journey is hardly a novelty. The point for me is that the tapestry demands that I travel. It is so engaging a work, so truthful a commentary on my life, that I cannot ignore its summons. It beckons to me, this Christian magic carpet; it says, come travel with me, pursue this vision of glory, glimpse things that hitherto you had only dreamt about; only don't stand still, as if God did not have more light and truth to reveal, more dimensions of goodness and love to make known to his children.

I am thinking as I write this of my own experience of how travel stretches the mind and imagination. Usually, as I have said, it is some specific goal that is the reason for travelling, even if all we can do is put a name to a destination and point to it on a map. For some reason that even now I cannot fully understand, I was fascinated as a young boy by boundaries between districts, counties or countries. Crossing by car from Middlesex into Hertfordshire on a family day out took on the romantic aspect of visiting another land. Hertfordshire was foreign territory to me. In my mind's eye, I imagined customs posts by the boundary signs, changes of language, currency and custom. One day, shortly before my ninth birthday, I resolved that I would cross this magic line on my own, and penetrate deep within the terrain on the other side. So I mounted my cycle, waved goodbye to my mother, and headed up the pavements of the Great North Road (could a youngster choose to be brought up near a more romantically named road?) Hours later, with great elation I reached the sacred place. There was early blossom in the hedgerows, I recall, and I picked some to take back with me as if it were a pilgrim's token. Honour satisfied, I turned round and retraced the hard-won miles back home, where I was mightily surprised to find the police out looking for me.

I recall that far-off March day as vividly now as I experienced it then. But I sense a meaning in this odyssey of mine that I did not see at the time. There seems to be a parable in it of life as growing up and growing away: leaving the safety of 'home', making a slow, sometimes arduous, even risky, journey in order to 'cross over' into another country, a new place. Perhaps it was a kind of rite of passage, a somewhat precocious but nevertheless important symbolic statement of needing to make my own journey, rather than have it wished on me by others. Perhaps I was testing other kinds of 'boundaries' – those imposed by parental authority for instance. If only life's journey were always charged with such exhilaration and excitement. Mostly it is a matter of the routine and ordinary, when it is as if we are becalmed, not going anywhere, those times of 'inconsistancy, boredom, anxiety' as Pascal describes the human condition.[3] Yet, as we have all experienced at certain times of our lives, they can be; and very probably, it is at times of greatest movement in our lives, greatest change, however painful, that in fact we feel most alive.

The tapestry then, becomes for me a magic carpet of infinite and wonderful possibilities. It invites me to 'cross over' my bounded little world and experience something new, something that transcends what I have known up to now. And this 'crossing over', this pilgrimage, is not fantasy, though imagination will have a large part to play in it. For the journey I make in prayer and meditation as I stand before the tapestry is a movement I must live out in life. The journey must touch my ordinary days. It is not that there is a 'real' world of everyday life that is somehow more real than prayer and meditation; simply that the two must connect, intersect each other if both are to be about what lies at the centre of being human and being Christian. The magic carpet is no escape from reality. On the contrary, it is a flight into it.

FLYING INTO REALITY

The story from the *Arabian Nights* has an ending that illustrates this. All three gifts brought by the sons in the Sultan's competition are judged to be equally wonderful: the magic looking glass, the magic apple, the magic carpet. So the Sultan sets another test for his sons. This time, Husain loses. So he renounces the world and his own claim to the throne, and becomes a dervish, living in the desert in great simplicity and dedicating his life to Allah the compassionate. In other words, because of the carpet, Husain decides to leave the 'fantasy' world of riches, power and idleness, and take up the life of renunciation and simplicity. In the desert, and stripped now of illusion, he encounters God. The carpet has led him straight to the heart of reality.

'Everything begins with mysticism and ends with politics' says the French poet and thinker Charles Peguy.[4] The tapestry helps me learn this lesson that mysticism – the spiritual life and politics – the life of involvement in the world's affairs – are not different. Contemplation and action are the two sides of this one journey. 'Christ in Glory' draws me into glory too. That is journey's end: our human destiny is to be like him. But it is also, as St Paul says, a journey 'from glory to glory'[5]: from one degree of glory to another. And that glory is as much manifested on the roadside, so to speak, as in the destination. 'Christ in Glory' comes to me in the here and now as well as in the not yet; in the rough and tumble of politics as well as in the ecstasy of mystical experience; in serving the world as well as worshipping God. The journey is more than getting to a destination. It has a validity of its own.

And that is important if I am to be open to the new things I believe lie around the corner. I must not lose my child's ability to catch my breath in wonder at the unexpected, to celebrate surprise, to be delighted at the unknown realms into which the magic carpet wings me. The tapestry makes a traveller of me. But I must not have too many preconceptions about where this journey is going to take me, nor how it will change me. 'God of surprises' is how he is, and always will be. And that is what ensures that this journey, whatever else may come of it, will at least be eventful. That is why it promises to be a movement into meaning: the very meaning of life, of truth, of God himself.

IN A SENSE, AMBIGUOUS

I have thought of this book as a piece of travel writing, a spiritual Baedeker. The journey I am describing is my own journey around the tapestry, or perhaps I should say, my journey into the tapestry, across it. For as I embark on this voyage, I soon realise that, as I have said, it is going to take me into new realms of experience, demand of me that I reflect truthfully on my life, ask myself questions that at times may be painful and hard. Only in this way will I come to a new longing for God, a new yearning that his love may be more really embodied within me, in my work, my leisure, my relationships, my suffering, my joy. As every traveller finds, who bothers to think at all about the significance of travel, this adventure turns out to he an exploration of meanings, a journey into the self. As a Christian, I want to say that such a journey is always also a journey of the spirit, a journey into God. I cannot travel, and not be changed in some way. So, as I journey through the great work of art that is the tapestry of Christ in Glory, I find that some mysterious grace is at work, gently but insistently helping me to see, to understand, to embrace life as the pure gift of God, and then to play my part in sharing that abundant, God-given life in the world of human life and endeavour.

In this book, then, I am describing a landscape. The landscape of the tapestry is its rich symbolism: the colours, the figures, the patterns and their interconnectedness. To some extent, I am describing what is there, what every eye can see, although art critics and historians will not be much helped by my commentary. Far more important, I think, is that I am trying to put into words what I see. That may not be what you see, and it may not even be what the artist himself intended us to see (if an artist is ever rash enough to prescribe what others might or should see in his or her work). Like a travel writer, I am simply setting out what this symbolic landscape means to me, how I experience it, how it touches and interprets life.

In a way, the true landscape is not the art work of the tapestry. It is life itself: my life, yours, our common life as human beings, as a planet. And so, all I can say is that this is how I see it. You may want to stand alongside me and see it in a similar way yourself; or you may see it in an entirely different way, your own unique way, the way that is personal to you.

Perhaps that is better, more honest. No two people make entirely the same journey, see in entirely the same way. This freedom to see what I see is an important and liberating one. The French stained-glass window makers at Chartres call it by the suggestive name of *tolérance*. It is a way of saying that in our encounter with truth, each of us must do his or her own work if there is to be an authentic vision, some new breakthrough into seeing things in a new, more vivid, way. When Kierkegaard said that 'truth is subjectivity', he meant that there is no avoiding that inward, personal struggle that has to be lived through if truth is to be made one with life. And this, too, is what he meant by the catch phrase he gave as the title of one of his books: *Purity of Heart is to Will One Thing*[6]: to see things in such a way, to experience them so vividly, to integrate them so committedly into the totality of my experience that truth and life fuse into one reality. The German poet Rilke spoke of *Herzwerk*, of doing 'heart work on the images within you'. That is what this book is: an exploration of the tapestry's symbols and images that will lead to 'heart work' that is life-changing and discloses God.

'Nearly everything in the design is in a sense ambiguous,'[7] writes Graham Sutherland about his own work. All art is like that, all writing, all music, all preaching. 'Ambiguous', in the sense of going both ways, taking in the landscape both to right and to left. I need both my right eye and my left to see things with depth, see below the surface as it were. 'Ambiguity', in that sense, is a good word, an inclusive one. It refuses to say that any one viewpoint is the only one, or the best.[8] It acknowledges that every vantage point brings its richness to bear upon the scene. So, 'heart work' will entail 'going both ways', so that the landscape is seen stereoscopically, as it were, with depth and perspective.

Making Theologians Of Us

So the landscape of the tapestry leads me into the landscape of my own life. I have chosen to write in the first person singular, and, where it seems appropriate, to tell something of my own story as a human being coming to terms with the love of God in Christ. This may make what I have to say seem very individualistic, over personal. A risk of all religion, as of any enterprise of therapy or personal growth, is that we become obsessed with our own selves and the tales we have to tell. Yet, paradoxically, this is the very mistake that the tapestry helps me not to make. For I see it as a properly universal work of art, an icon of the church's life, an image of the world. It teaches me to say 'we' as well as 'I'. It addresses what we have in common: our condition, the 'joy and woe' that are 'woven fine'[9] in the life of the human race. It is, then, about politics as well as prayer, about society as well as sacraments, about mission as well as meditation. It is about all these things, because Christ in Glory is the Lord of them all.

I can sum all this up by saying that the tapestry makes *theologians* out of us. It does that by addressing to us the central issues of our lives, the 'grail-questions' as I shall call them later on: what it means to be human, what it means to live together, and what it means to do these things in God. A theologian is someone who talks about God, that is, reflects on meanings in the light of faith and tries to make sense of a world in which God is believed to be present and involved. We become theologians, the Orthodox Christians of the east would say, not by reading books, or even by *thinking* at all, but through worship and prayer, through the living experience of God. To that extent, every Christian is a theologian. I like to imagine the tapestry drawing out of people their innate theological instincts. That is what it does for me.

And it is because I am an ordinary human being, struggling to understand the Christian life in a confusing world, that I have dared to say 'I' as well as 'we'. It is what we have in common that makes me think that from 'I' it is but a short step to 'we'. The landscape is the landscape of us all.

3
TRAVELLING COMPANIONS

THE TAPESTRY, as I have said, makes a traveller out of me. It is a journey only I can make. As a human being, as a Christian, the voyage is mine alone. No-one else can make it for me, and I cannot make it for anyone else.

There is something a little frightening about this. The thought of a lifelong voyage into the unknown, with its choices, risks, uncertainties, dangers, could make me feel quite queasy if I dwelt on it. I understand, very often, that traditional Breton fisherman's prayer: 'Lord, the sea is so big, and my boat is so small'. Yet there is something glorious about it as well. Human life, for all its tragedy and pathos, is profoundly heroic. I stand on the brink of the unknown, and, alongside the queasiness, I feel an elation of the spirit. Something rises up within me, and I know I was born for this. Matthew Arnold put it like this:

> A wanderer is man from his birth.
> He was born in a ship
> On the breast of the River of Time.[1]

Much of the time I am lethargic, listless. I would rather stay in the harbour where the waters are calm and shallow, and the landscape is familiar. But I know, in my heart, that this is not yet where I am meant to be. I must leave those familiar, secure shores, and head for the open sea. 'O daring joy, but safe! are they not all the seas of God?'[2] asks Walt Whitman, as he contemplates the mystery, often dark and brooding, of the wide ocean. 'O farther, farther, farther sail!' This, for me, is what religion is about. It is not to protect me against life's storms, but to give me the courage to weigh anchor, take on the ocean and face them. Philip Toynbee, in his journal, quotes a friend who becomes a parish priest. 'I wanted a job where I couldn't feel the bottom.'[3] The best spiritual voyages are those where the fathoms are deep beneath our feet.

BREAD-SHARING

Only I can make this journey. But I am not alone. I have travelling companions, many of them. One of the joys of travelling is to compare notes, share experiences, look at one another's maps, tell stories. I see the church as a community of fellow travellers, a pilgrim people. The liturgy is one of those places where I am helped to feel I am not alone. A 'companion' is literally someone who shares your bread with you.[4] The church is, as the Prayer Book calls us, 'the blessed company of all faithful people' – a body of bread-sharers. At the eucharist, I share bread with my friends, and am strengthened to journey on.

And the liturgy brings me into a wider company of friends than those I can know and love personally. There are the writers of the Bible themselves, through whose words I hear the word of God. There are those who lovingly (as I want to believe) devised the liturgy, created its texts, wrote prayers and hymns and even rubrics. There are those generations of believing men and women who have prayed this same liturgy before me, breathed heaven into its bones, made its prayer valid. And there are the saints, the angels, the archangels, 'all the company of heaven' says the *Sanctus*. All of these, in the poetry of the liturgy, attend the celebration. It is a rich fellowship to be in.

But then there are the artists, craftspeople, poets, musicians, whose creative skills adorn our worship. And these, I want to suggest, are more than travelling companions. They are, in an important sense, guides. Along with the biblical writers, it is the artists to whom I owe most in the direction my journey has taken. It is as if these men and women, these explorers of the human spirit before me, have bequeathed me with maps, charts, experiences that help me to navigate. Their stories are not mine, of course. But they can assist me to find my own way. I owe them a tremendous debt.

THE EYES OF OTHERS

This is what I mean when I say that the tapestry stirs me from within and makes me want to travel. Graham Sutherland's artistic vision has a profound effect on me. As a work of art, the tapestry beckons me, as all great art should do, to see things in a new way, to share the artist's vision. Can I glimpse what he has glimpsed? Can I go with him?

Of course, I cannot help seeing the world through the eyes of others. Sometimes it is for better, sometimes for worse. I can think of several occasions when a work of art has changed my perception of things. Almost (not quite) the first piece of music to kindle my imagination was Schubert's song cycle *Die Winterreise* 'The Winter's Journey'. Its portrait, in song, of a forlorn young man, disappointed in love, making his lonesome journey across the frozen landscape has haunted me ever since. Winter for me means these poems of Müller and the music of Schubert. Come the first frosts, and I can see that journey leading away from warmth and light into the icy nightmare of oblivion.

In the same way, the first page of Dickens' novel *Bleak House*, a matchless description of 'implacable November weather' has coloured my thoughts about autumn ever since I was given it to copy out as handwriting practice at school. In spring and summer I see the English countryside through the eyes of Constable, and hear its sounds through the ears of Vaughan-Williams. The landscape of childbirth means the poetry of Traherne, and of death, Tennyson's *In Memoriam*. In a more explicitly religious context (but I count all of these as religious in the sense that ultimately matters), I believe it was singing the treble line in Bach's *St John Passion* over a quarter of a century ago that brought me face to face with the cross in a decisive way. The cross has been central to my faith ever since.

So, Sutherland's tapestry is one more window on to reality. It draws me into its own vision, its own life. In the next chapter, I shall explore the language of icons to help explain how I see this. But it is important to me to see all art, all human creativity, as somehow acting as a 'vade-mecum', inviting me to explore part of reality more deeply, whether it is God, the world or myself. And, as I hope to explain, the tapestry is for me a marvellous entering into reality at these three levels: God, the world and myself. It is a good companion for the journey.

VIRGIL AND BEATRICE

This idea of art as a travelling companion and guide first came alive for me when I set myself the task some years back of reading through Dante's *Divine Comedy*. There was more than a sense of duty about this. Symbolically, I decided to read the *Inferno* and the *Purgatorio* during Lent, and tackle the *Paradiso* (if I ever got that far) in Eastertide. I admit that I was staggered by the beauty and vitality of Dante's writing, even in translation[5]; his brilliant exploration of the human psyche; his insights into the meaning of judgement and salvation; the ruthless honesty with which he probes the meaning of life, death and destiny. It was an extraordinarily powerful experience to live in the company of this incomparably great mind during those days.

Dante's vision is based on the idea of a journey. Lost in the midst of a thick, trackless forest 'in the middle of the road of our life',[6] a guide comes to Dante's aid. That first stanza contains enough food for thought for anyone in a time of change or transition looking both backwards and forwards, reassessing goals and re-evaluating priorities. At such times, I need a guide, a friend to lead me through the thicket of choices and decisions I face, to help me maintain any sense of direction. Dante's guide on his journey is the Roman poet Virgil. He leads him around the circle of hell, and then up the slopes of Mount Purgatory beyond. It is an epic voyage.

Dante seems to be saying that the poet (who can stand for the artist in any medium) can help me to see what I may prefer to avoid: the judgement, the hell, those great refusals (as Dante calls human sin) that are so destructively at work in so much of human life: and in my own life too. The poet, the painter, the musician can, like the Old Testament prophet, point out what is wrong in life and how it needs to be put right and healed. The poetry of Wilfred Owen, for instance, uttered a cry of protest against the Great War that was conspicuously lacking on the lips of church men and women.[7] Picasso's painting *Guernica* (which Sutherland calls 'the major religious work of the twentieth century'[8]) and Benjamin Britten's *War Requiem* (first performed in the newly consecrated Coventry Cathedral in 1962) also seem to me to fulfil this Virgil-like role. They expose what is bitter, painful and demonic. They guide me around hell in order to lead me up through purgatory towards the place of salvation.

Beyond purgatory, Dante is given a new guide, the immortal Beatrice. She is his personification of beauty, who leads him through the glories of heaven to the vision of God himself, whom Dante calls 'the love that moves the sun and the other stars'.[9]

Beatrice, to me, represents the other side of art. She stands for the element of beauty and happiness in it, its ability to lift our spirits, offer us visions. Just as Virgil epitomises the truthful element in art, Beatrice symbolises all that is lovely, all that redeems and makes whole. Together, Virgil and Beatrice interpret to me the entire human condition: our hell, our purgatory, our heaven. I learn, with the help of these guides, where this journey of life is leading me. Their charts plot its places of safety and danger. At their hands, I feel safe enough to travel on.

All this is a way of saying that the tapestry, as art, will lead me somewhere if I am prepared to surrender myself to it, and see what it sees. For me, it has something of that universal quality of *The Divine Comedy* about it. I see it as reflecting those same great human themes of death, judgement, hell and heaven; of life and suffering and love. It is not beautiful at the expense of truth, nor is it truthful at the expense of beauty. It is both Virgil and Beatrice. I sink down to hell, on the cross below; and I soar to heaven in the light above. Supremely, I am drawn to Christ, the Lord of both hell and heaven. I meet in him the love that moves the sun and the other stars.

LIT BY THE IMAGINATION

I do not need to be told that there is a danger lurking in all this. I need to remember that the last sounds heard by some of those who perished in Auschwitz, other than their own cries for help, were of Mozart and Haydn and Beethoven. I need to remember that some of the world's most beautiful countries are also places of deep division and conflict: as I write, the example of Tibet comes to mind, or what we used to call Yugoslavia, or Ireland. Beauty does not by itself redeem. I must not reduce religion to an aesthetic experience, as if it were no more than art or civilisation tinged with emotion, to parody Matthew Arnold. That would make religion elitist, an activity for the cultured few. Precisely that fault is present in some of the more rarified forms of Christian worship I come across from time to time, not least in cathedrals.

So, why do I need to insist so strongly on the role of art as guiding us into the truth and beauty that is God? Are not Moses and St. Paul sufficient, without needing Virgil and Beatrice as well?

I can only answer this at a personal level. For me, it all comes down to that neglected God-given faculty, the imagination. I ask myself how my imagination is going to be activated into generous thoughts of God, visions of redeeming love, fervent resolve to throw myself into the world's struggles and claim it as Christ's own? Emily Dickinson talks about the open windows of possibility:

I dwell in Possibility –
A fairer House than Prose.[10]

Poetry, she is saying, leads to 'the spreading wide my narrow Hands to gather Paradise'. Elsewhere, she speaks about 'the Possible's slow fuse lit by the imagination'.

That seems to me to have been the instinct of most religious people from earliest times: to clothe the words of religious faith with visual images, movement and music, in other words to open up a passage to the heart via any and all of the senses with which we human beings are endowed.

A pilgrimage to Rome as a student helped me to see the importance of this. A friend and I spent two weeks in that marvellous city, discovering its classical and baroque splendours. We saw everything we could in that short time, and loved it all. Yet it was too much to take in at one time, like downing neat spirit too quickly. I felt heady, intoxicated with art. I longed for a way of making sense of what I had experienced, of integrating it somehow, so that, rather than emerge from the celestial city in some kind of drunken aesthetic stupor, I might perhaps be helped to see life more clearly as a result of being there.

Towards the end of our fortnight, we visited the Catacombs. After all that we had seen, it was like a glass of clear, cold water. In the dark, holy place I felt touched, moved in a way in which the Vatican, for all its magnificence, had not quite succeeded in doing. For me, there are not many places as 'thin' as the Catacombs, as transparent to God and the grace of life. On the walls of the Catacombs, I saw those amazing frescoes from the earliest Christian centuries: Jonah, Daniel, Noah; the wedding at Cana, the feeding of the crowd. Here, it seemed to me, were the meditations, prayers and longings of those fervent believers breathed into visible, tangible form. Like prehistoric cave paintings, there was something deeply affecting in the naïve simplicity of this art so charged with love and devotion. They were a kind of commentary on the biblical text that had passed through the lives and prayers of those who had painted them. Perhaps, even, you might say that the lives of those early Christians were the true text, and the Bible and the paintings the commentary.

This clarifies for me that everything serves the same end – the knowledge of God. The scriptures, the Christian inheritance of faith, what we call the 'tradition' have a cherished part to play in that path to the knowledge of God – at least, they do for me. But perhaps the artist, the poet, the novelist, the playwright and the musician can help me to break the ecclesiastical seal on it, prise it open a little and expose its riches. They can cast new light on what is old, and perhaps too familiar. Once, at story time just before going to bed, one of my children asked to be read some parables. So we worked through some of St. Luke's. And because this was the hour for fantasy and fairy-tales, I not only found myself reading the parables aloud in a new way, I also rediscovered something of their freshness and vitality. It had done us both good to lift them out of the formally religious context into a setting where we were free to see and hear new things. That in itself is a small parable of what I mean.

All this, of course, is to affirm and celebrate the work of human hands. There is an important truth here, or rather a cluster of important truths: the goodness of the material world; the privilege of being human and having been given the faculty of creativity; the Incarnation, affirming both material things and human involvement with them. The creation story in Genesis speaks not only of God the all-powerful bringer-out-of-nothing. It also celebrates God the craftsman, infinitely carefully fashioning, sculpting his handiwork, making of the world something fit to be called a work of art. The craftspeople, those who work with their hands, 'maintain the fabric of the world',[11] says the Old Testament in a striking metaphor we might have thought applicable only to God. And this warns me against seeing 'art' in too narrow a way. My guides may be anything that speak to me as Virgil and Beatrice: grand opera or soap opera; tapestry or newspaper cartoon; string quartet or heavy metal; a gothic cathedral or a well-laid dining table. . . It is up to me to find art all around me, and allow it to lead me where it will.

HEART SPEAKS TO HEART

Vita Sackville-West, in her poem *Craftsmen*, has a wonderful image of what I mean:

All craftsmen share a knowledge. They have held
Reality down fluttering to a bench.[12]

Art encompassing life, holding reality down like a fluttering bird cupped, for a time, between the hands: that picture speaks to me about things I grasp best by seeing, touching, holding. In that way, the words of faith are made flesh, given sacramental power. I find they begin to speak to the whole of me. Is that why Beethoven prefaced the score of his *Missa Solemnis* with the telling words: 'From the heart; may it go to the heart'?

Heart speaking to heart, reality held between the hands, long enough to feel its throbbing life before it flies free of us again?

I contemplate the great tapestry, and feel there is a rightness about this way of thinking: 'cor ad cor loquitur'[13] 'The heart has its own reasons of which reason knows nothing'[14] said Pascal wisely. If he was right then, in his own 17th century, how much more right is he today, in an age increasingly preoccupied with what is explainable and rational? I need the tapestry to bring my whole humanity into play: all its God-given faculties for understanding and appreciating, for enjoying and celebrating, for wondering and longing.

And then, paradoxically, I feel that the universe is somehow within reach.

4

ICON: IMAGE AND PRESENCE

I FIRST saw the tapestry at the age of twelve. Coventry Cathedral was consecrated in May 1962. With millions of other people, my parents decided we should see the new building. Part of the appeal of this trip was to motor up from London on the newly opened M1. Both the Cathedral and the motorway seemed then, in their different ways, to stand for something important in the revitalised, confident Britain of the early 1960s; both the journey and the destination, as I look back on it, symbolised a Britain putting the struggles of the past behind her, and eagerly embracing the promise of the new.

That day indeed turned out to hold the promise of the new for me personally. I had expected to find the motorway exciting, and was prepared to be politely interested in the Cathedral. In the event, this journey proved to be one of those surprising ones I wrote about in the second chapter. I was overwhelmed by the Cathedral. The great baptistry window, the Chapel of Christ in Gethsemane, the jet-black marble floor – in those days like a deep pool in which you could see your own reflection – I knew I should never forget the impact these all made on me.

But more than anything else, it was the tapestry that conquered me: great and green and full of things that I could barely guess at, yet that filled me with a sense of joy. It made me sit down in the centre of the nave and look at it. In those days, the Cathedral was seething with visitors; yet I do not remember being surrounded by people. My memory is of being entirely alone, of there being only two realities in that moment of meeting: the tapestry, and me. It was my first consciously 'religious' experience.

DOORS OF PERCEPTION

Conversion, I now realise, is a long process, a lifelong one. At various points on the road, we pass milestones and know that there is movement. It was some years later that the 'penny dropped' and I was baptised a Christian. But I owe much to Graham Sutherland's tapestry. I think it opened, or began to open, what Blake calls the 'doors of perception'. Like blind Bartimaeus, in St Mark's story[1], I not only began to *see*, but also to trust, to follow Jesus 'on the way'. For me, the tapestry proved more than a picture. It proved an icon.

The Greek word *eikon* simply means 'image'. That word – 'image' – is a word I find myself using a lot, probably because of the cognate word 'imagination'. An image, it seems to me, requires imagination if it is to come alive. I can look at an image – a painting, a photograph, a piece of sculpture, a story, a symbol or a poem – and I can respond to it in two ways. I can see it as two-dimensional, all surface and no depth; I then think I have exhausted its meaning and turn away. Or I can come to grasp it as three-dimensional, as having an infinite number of facets, a life of its own. Then its depth and possibilities become inexhaustible. Its own reality begins to encounter mine and probe it; there is a meeting of its life and mine.

One of the holy places of England for me is Bemerton, once a small village just outside Salisbury, now a suburb of that city. I recall that my family and I had not lived in Wiltshire for more than twenty-four hours when I cycled out to Bemerton through the industrial estates of Salisbury. Here in the 17th century lived and worked one of that great succession of poet-parsons, George Herbert, who was its incumbent from 1630 to 1633. It was a brief incumbency in a short life, as his first biographer puts it, 'a life so full of charity, humility, and all Christian virtues that it deserves the eloquence of St Chrysostom to commend and declare it'.[2]

In the tiny dark church of Bemerton, dwarfed by its own vicarage, holiness became almost tangible in the prayer and writing of one of our greatest metaphysical poets. In any poetry, perhaps image and metaphor are all; but especially is this true of Herbert. His poem 'The Elixir' is well-known as a hymn. It is primarily about 'sweeping a room as for God's laws': make drudgery divine, and heaven breaks out. But it is equally as good an encapsulation of how words and art become bearers of divine meanings, sacraments of what is beyond our grasp:

> A man that looks on glass,
> On it may stay his eye.
> Or if he pleaseth, through it pass,
> And then the heaven espy.[3]

That is where the imagination comes in. It breathes life into words, representations, objects so that they become living images, icons – just as God breathed into the flesh and bones of the first human, so that he became a living, responding person, able to carry and express, in his own being, the image of his Maker.

Samuel Johnson talks about 'hunger of imagination',[4] a kind of divine discontent that expands our horizons and enables us, not only to dream dreams, but begin to make those dreams reality. And if that is how wheels are invented, Mount Everest conquered, and tuberculosis cured, then patently, we cannot live without it. I am coming to believe that without imagination of the spirit, the soul too will wither away and die. I am at my most listless, least aware, when the imaginative faculty within me lies dormant, unexercised. George Herbert's metaphor for this truth is that of the pulley. In his poem of that name, God pours out upon humanity a 'glass of blessings': beauty, wisdom, honour and pleasure. At the end, only one blessing is left to bestow: rest. This gift he withholds, for it is the one that will entice human beings to their Maker:

> Yet let him keep the rest,
> But keep them with repining restlessness:
> Let him be rich and weary, that at least,
> If goodness lead him not, yet weariness
> May toss him to my breast.[5]

It was St Anselm who expounded the argument that God, the Being 'than whom nothing greater can be conceived', must necessarily exist, because otherwise he would be less than perfect. A God who exists, he is saying, is 'greater' than one who doesn't, therefore, he must exist. This so-called 'ontological' argument is difficult to follow, and philosophers still debate whether it makes sense as a logical deduction. But as I read Anselm afresh, and realise that it was, for him, a matter not of *coming to* faith, but of 'faith seeking understanding',[6] I begin to grasp the point. He was, I think, appealing to *imagination* rather than thought. He was saying, in effect, let the imagination stretch my mind to conceive the inconceivable; and then let it pull me into relationship with it, so that what I begin to *imagine*, I also begin to *glimpse*, and then to *know* and to *love*. That is what the icon invites me to do; and the tapestry also. They are pulleys, tugging away at my imagination until I surrender and see God.

THE UNVEILING

So an icon, in the narrow, technical sense of the word, is more than merely a picture, even a religious picture. It is rather a kind of presence, a sacrament glowing with a divine life of its own. I look at an icon of Christ, or the Virgin Mary, or the saints, and I see more than simply a representation. It is as if the subject of the icon is manifested to me in some direct way, so that I cease to be a spectator and become instead a worshipper. My imaginative prayer and attention, focused on the icon, allow it to become a vehicle of grace to me. My doors of perception are opened. Through the door of the icon I glimpse another world. I glimpse what, in my 'ordinary' life tends to remain hidden: the company of angels and saints, the presence of Christ, the rule of God himself.

We could use the language of unveiling to describe this experience of being allowed to peer within the mystery of life. It is striking that St Mark's Gospel begins and ends with the idea that in Jesus, there is an unveiling, a revelation of what was hidden from human sight. At Jesus' baptism, we are told, the sky was 'torn apart' as the Spirit descended upon him, and the voice from heaven thundered its approval: 'You are my Son, the beloved'.[7] But at the crucifixion, Mark returns to the same word to describe how the temple curtain was 'torn in two' as Jesus cried out and breathed his last.[8] It is at this moment of tearing apart that the centurion recognises Jesus for what he is: 'Truly this man was God's Son!' In Jesus then, as the man from God, something final is disclosed to the world, unveiled, both in his coming amongst us to proclaim good news, and also (Mark would say supremely) in the paradox of the cross. The gospel story is itself an icon in words. It draws me into its own movement of grace. It changes me.

ICONS AND LOVE

An icon, traditionally, is an act of love. It is loved in the making, loved in the praying, and speaks of divine love active in the world. A true icon is never a mere reproduction (still less a photograph) of someone else's work. Despite the traditions within which icon-painters work, it is always the unique offering of some individual artist, his or her worship as well as work. No two icons are ever the same. And although we know the identities of a few famous icon-painters, most are without name. For the focus of an icon is the mystery of God alone. It is as if not even the name of the painter must be allowed to distract attention from the spiritual task for which the icon has been created.

We have at home a large icon of the birth of Christ painted – who knows when? – in the Byzantine tradition of the 14th and 15th centuries. This icon of ours conflates the entire Christmas story in one landscape: Mary, Joseph, the angels, the shepherds, the magi, the cattle, and right in the centre, wrapped in a winding sheet, the infant Jesus. It is a naïve painting, with little subtlety and not much artistic instinct. Yet it is a touching work. Some obscure man (or woman) spent many days creating it as an act of love. And the image of the tiny patch of white amid the reds, blues and golds – this born-to-die baby Jesus – often makes me stop and ponder as I pass the icon several times a day. We honour this icon at Christmas by decorating it with holly and ivy, and lighting all the candles we can find in front of it. Its homely glow sanctifies our Christmas celebrations, for Christ himself seems present. I am drawn into its world and something in me is touched and healed.

In Russia, recently, I saw for myself just how icons light up human lives. It was very moving to see them once again so lovingly prayed in front of by crowds of worshippers surging in apparently at every hour of the day. In every one of them I saw old women, the *baboushkas*, and guessed they were the backbone of Russia. They looked, some of them, as if they were as ancient as the churches themselves. With incredible devotion and sometimes courage, they had maintained the daily prayer of those empty shrines, unloved through seventy years of communism. I wondered whether they ever dreamed to see them full once more. I walked too a long way through the dusty Moscow streets in order to see the world-famous icons in the museums. Tourists crossed themselves in front of Rublev's marvellous icon of the Holy Trinity in the Tetryakov Museum, and I found it almost unbearable to drag myself away from its serene image of God being homely and intimate with us.

But what I recall even more vividly is something that happened in Moscow's Arbat, a street to which all tourists are drawn like a magnet for its street market. There you can buy souvenirs, second-hand books, ice-cream, antiques – almost anything, including icons. For it is a sad fact of modern Russian life that so poor are the majority of the population, so desperate are they for money enough to buy food, drink and shelter, that even the household icons, loved and cared for over generations, are being sold off to dealers with an eye for a quick gain at the tourist's expense.

I had no wish to take an icon out of its homeland. I felt strongly that they belonged in Russia and that, in some mystical way, as long as they remained there, there was hope yet for a land suffering so desperately the hardships I saw all around me. But as I stopped by an icon stall, a young man came up, and prostrated himself in front of the icons piled up higgledy-piggledy on the trestle table. After a minute or two, he began, infinitely carefully, to pick up the icons in turn, kiss them and then replace them on the table so that no icon obscured the image of the ones below. Then, once again, he knelt on the pavement and worshipped silently. The tourists gaped; but this worshipper was oblivious to us, just as I had been oblivious to the crowds on my first encounter with the tapestry. It was as if he inhabited a reality of his own; and I dare to think that it was he, and not the rest of us, who were closest to reality just then. It was a kind of transfiguration amid a city street.

This is what I mean when I call the tapestry an icon: not technically, but in the way it functions. Unlike my icon at home, the tapestry is consciously art, and art of a high order. But it seems to me that it is more even than great art. When visitors who have never seen it before and who may in fact find it perplexing, say that the face of Christ follows them round the Cathedral, it is this icon-like aspect of it they are experiencing. The tapestry is more than a beautiful decoration: it is a presence, a gateway to another world, a sacrament of divine love. Attend to it with loving imagination, and it draws me into its life, changing my perspectives, clarifying my goals. It speaks to me of God.

How the tapestry speaks to me of God is what this book is about. I have already explained that I use the first person pronoun deliberately, for I can write only of how it speaks to me. The icon deals personally with each of us. It is not a question of whether what I see is what the artist intended one to see. It is simply what is there for me; what, if you like, is God's gift to me through it; and that is as unique to me as the artist's or painter's vision was to him or her. In the letter to the church at Pergamum, one of the seven churches of Asia to whom John the Divine wrote, there is a lovely personal touch that I relish: 'To everyone who conquers . . . I will give a white stone, and on the white stone is written a new name that no-one knows except the one who receives it'.[9] That is how it is when I meditate on the tapestry, or admire a Picasso or read the Bible, or listen to Mozart. There is that unique, personal meeting between it and me, that gift with my own name upon it.

THE MYSTERY OF OURSELVES

There is one more point about an icon. 'Image' can mean a reflected image: the icon can be a mirror as well as a doorway. I have already suggested that the journey into God is also a journey into myself. So I should not be surprised to find that I see myself in an icon: myself as I am, myself as I might become. Loving attention to the icon may mean paying loving attention not only to God, but also to my own soul. I have already alluded to the oracle that still speaks to us out of that place to which souls in search once resorted, Delphi: 'know yourself'. A true knowing of God will always go hand in hand with a true knowing of my own human condition.

I remember, one Ash Wednesday, spending a conducted Quiet Day with my colleagues. Our leader invited each of us to choose an icon out of many she had brought with her, and to spend the day with it. I chose an icon of the boy Jesus in the temple with the elders and teachers. At first this icon, attractive enough as art, said very little to me, until we were asked to meditate on how we saw ourselves in our icon. At once I saw my situation mirrored – my work with colleagues considerably my senior in age and experience, my own preoccupation, unhealthy at times, with status and position, my envy of those who achieve so much so young. But I saw too, in a new way, that in that temple scene, both the experience of age and the freshness of youth are affirmed. I went back to Luke's story,[10] and read it more carefully. I discovered that the young Jesus and the teachers listened to each other, it seems, with respect and openness. They were all willing to learn. I thought about our staff team, and resolved to celebrate the rich diversity of age and experience represented there, my own contribution among them. The mirror had told the truth in a healing, redeeming way.

As I worship in the Cathedral with the tapestry above, I see myself in it as well as Christ. Explicitly, I am there in the diminutive figure of the man between the feet of Christ. But I am there implicitly in the rest of it too, if I have eyes to see. For the tapestry is an icon of the story of Christ; and what is the story of Christ but my own story of life, death, resurrection and glory? Just as in the four gospels, so here. I see in the agony and ecstasy of Christ my own agony and ecstasy. 'It is the mystery of ourselves that is on the altar', says St. Augustine of the Eucharist. It is the same truth: 'Your life is hid with Christ in God', says St. Paul.[11] *His* and *mine* merge. They become one and the same: 'Christ in you, the hope of glory'.[12]

THE LIFE OF THINGS

Sometimes, in summer, when the sun shines in bars of light across the tapestry, I have the illusion that it is not really part of the Cathedral at all, but is beyond it somewhere, and I am looking out at it through a great window. Then, fleetingly, it is as if the tapestry is a world outside, green and gold and red with the strong colours of June. And in the midst, Christ.

It is a dream, of course. But it is a good one. For my work with icons has helped me to see that in an important way, the whole of creation is an icon, glowing with the presence of God its maker. It puts its own questions to us, asks us who we are and where we are going. So God silences Job, after the argument has gone round and round, by showing him the mysteries of creation and asking him how he responds. Job sees it as an icon: to see the world, truly to see it, is to see God, he seems to say. 'I had heard of you by the hearing of the ear, but now my eyes see you'.[13] So the psalmist finds himself searching after the truth of things in front of this icon: 'When I look at the heavens, the work of your fingers, the moon and the stars that you have established, what are human beings that you are mindful of them, mortals that you care for them?'[14] So the poet, in much-quoted but deeply felt lines:

> And I have felt
> A presence that disturbs me with the joy
> Of elevated thoughts: a sense sublime
> Of something far more deeply interfused,
> Whose dwelling is the light of setting suns,
> And the round ocean, and the living air,

> And the blue sky, and in the mind of man:
> A motion and a spirit that impells
> All thinking things, all objects of all thought,
> And rolls through all things.[15]

Wordsworth speaks of seeing 'into the life of things'. As I sensitise my imagination, learn to see the world as a sacrament, an icon, I begin to 'see into the life of things'. To do that, I discover, is to adopt a religious outlook on the world, on life. I reverence life more than I did, because I glimpse Christ at its centre, as he is at the heart of the tapestry.

And within the icon of the world, as Wordsworth's line about 'the mind of man' says, I see my fellow human beings. The psalm tells me that they are 'crowned with glory and honour'. I turn back to the creation story, and discover why. It is because they – you, I – are made as the image of God, his 'icon', says the Greek text. I look into the face of my brother and sister of any race, any culture, any religious faith or none. What I see is a living, moving icon. What I see is something of God himself.

I look back at the tapestry to help me make sense of this mystery. Like the visitor seeing it for the first time, my eyes return to the face of Christ in glory. I recall the words of the New Testament: how Christ 'is the image of the invisible God, the firstborn of all creation'.[16] There is the word again, 'image', literally 'icon'. He is the 'icon' par excellence, the archetypal icon to whom all other icons point. Our human lives, the created world, the arts, the icons of religion – Christ is the centre of them all. He interprets them all. All are sacraments of him. All radiate his presence. All are filled with the promise of glory to come, the day when Christ shall 'be all, in all'.

I 'see into the life of things', and feel that the vision of God cannot be far off.

5

WOVEN FINE

THE TAPESTRY is the work of many human hands, representing many different human skills. There is the art of its designer, the craft of those who wove it, the technology of those who made the loom, the science of those who created the dyes, the engineering of those who installed the tapestry in the Cathedral. I look at the tapestry and try to take in this fact that nothing is ever the work of one man or woman. The whole of life is a collaborative effort. We are members one of another.

This leads me to think about the actual process of weaving this immense carpet. Graham Sutherland tells us in his book about the tapestry, that it was important, for the integrity of the work, that it should be woven in one piece, rather than as separate segments subsequently stitched together. Only in France could this be done on such a scale, in the historic tapestry-making region around Aubusson on the river Creuse. I talk about the loom's 'technology'. The loom of the Pinton Frères at Felletin was 500 years old. Its rollers were 'two great tree-trunks weathered into gentleness by time'. During the weaving, only the narrow section of tapestry being worked on at the time was visible, the rest being hidden, wrapped around these primitive rollers. There were large notices in the workshop: 'la plus grande tapisserie du monde'.[1]

WARP AND WEFT

There is food for thought here. In this process of weaving a tapestry, I find a powerful metaphor of my life. It is no accident that we speak of 'life's rich tapestry', of 'the warp and weft of life'. Those phrases speak to me of life as a process rather than as a finished product. And it is a *process* that is the key to understanding life. As long as I am alive, I am in a constant process of *becoming*. From time to time I try to sum up what the story has been about. But I need mentally to write underneath the picture the words 'unfinished', 'provisional'. Both my successes and my failures make only partial sense as yet. More is to come. How much more I cannot know: how many more yards of warp are wrapped around the roller out of which to go on weaving life's tapestry. The fascination of my own life and other people's is this process by which what we are becoming is emerging out of what we already are: what undreamed-of possibilities are latent within what we already know and perceive about ourselves.

Tapestry is created out of warp and weft. The warp is the threads stretched out across the loom, ready for the weaver to cross them with the coloured weft. The warp is 'given'; the weft intersects with it at the behest of the weaver. Out of what is given, together with what is interwoven, emerges, very slowly and painstakingly, a work of art.

I see in this an eloquent picture of how my own life is created. I want to see the emergence of my life's story, not as something that merely 'happens', but as something that is created and purposeful, with its own beauty. I want my life to be a work of art. It helps me to think of the warp as what is 'given' to me, what is already 'there'. That will include my genes, my parenting, my early schooling, much of what befalls me in childhood. Over these I have little or no control. These threads are already strung across the loom. There are others too, which may only become evident later in life: illness, disability, accident or bereavement. This is the warp with which I must work creatively. The weft is, in my metaphor, what I do with those givens: the choices I make, the relationships I enter into, the extent to which I want to use even life's misfortunes as occasions for growth. The weft is my freedom to be the artist of my own life. It is that privilege that makes me a human being.

There is something very primitive in the idea that life is a kind of thread. In Greek mythology, the three Fates presided over the threads of human existence. Lachesis was held to spin life's thread and determine its length, Clotho to draw it off her distaff at the time of birth, and Atropos to cut it off at death. Other traditions say that at birth, the Fates bound the infant with swathing bands embroidered with the marks of family and clan, so determining the child's place in society. Lachesis means 'measurer'; Atropos means 'what cannot be avoided'; there is that which is already measured – determined for me, beyond my control. There is that which I cannot avoid.

But the myths are also clear that both gods and human beings had considerable freedom in the face of the Fates. Apollo once made them drunk to save his friend from death. There are things I can do something about. I can, out of the marks on my swathing bands, take charge of my destiny within the constraints of what is given. The warp is God's; the weft is mine. Life is both his and mine, the work of art a collaborative effort. I am co-worker with him. That gives my life its unique meaning and value. I learn to love God and do as I will, and make the marvellous discovery that my own joys and desires can become aligned to his.

Weaving a New World Order

All this of course applies equally to our common life. Our collective story as human beings, what we call 'history', is warp and weft too. There is that which is measured, and that which cannot he avoided for nations, societies and communities. The intractable dilemmas of our time are not wholly of our own conscious making. No-one set out to create mass unemployment, or the greenhouse effect. We are no doubt the heirs of our parents' and grandparents' unwitting sins. That has become for us what is given. What needs to be affirmed is that we can and must take control of our destiny. Christian faith says to me that the future is very largely our responsibility. What tapestry to weave, what picture to create, is the political and social question that faces us all.

I think, as I write these words, of the crises that are constantly in the news headlines, and are uppermost in our daily prayers. Refugees continue to stream out of the Bosnian villages in which they and their forebears have lived for centuries. The Russian dream of a modern, industrialised, democratic state emerging like a phoenix out of communism is fast disintegrating in the face of economic collapse. The far right in the new

Germany hurls firebombs at hostels where 'foreigners' are housed, and desecrates Jewish cemeteries. The killings in Ireland go on remorselessly while terrorist organisations shed crocodile tears of regret that innocent children suffer. Faced with this tragic mess we seem to have made of our continent, I ask myself what kind of world order will be needed to build the 'common European home' we heard so much about a few years ago. I ask what picture will be created here to replace the torn, tangled threads of this present confusion?

I need to resist the temptation to think I am powerless when it comes to the destinies of nations, and the future of my own society. For years, we have prayed, and others have struggled, for change in South Africa. The destiny of that country is something that I have felt personally since 1976. It was a glorious summer here in England. On Trinity Sunday, in an Oxford college chapel, I was ordained priest. On a radiantly beautiful evening, surrounded by the love of family and friends, I pledged that I would serve God and my neighbour as a minister in his church. Afterwards, we ate and drank on the college lawns. Oxford could not have been lovelier. Later that week, the world heard what had happened that day in a place many of us had never heard of – Soweto. Men, women and children had been killed, homes burned, a township raped. The contrast to an Oxford summer evening was awesome. And yet this was the world I lived in, the world my ordination committed me to serve.

I thought much of Soweto; I could not put out of my mind those poignant words that were the motto of those who campaigned for the end of the slave trade two hundred years ago: 'Am I not a man and a brother?' The green lawns of Oxford turned brown and parched as that scorching summer went on. What could I do but pray? Now, at last, we see the beginnings of prayer answered. South Africa is changing. The unfree are finding new freedoms. I am not powerless; and those who struggle are not powerless. I see spirituality as the weaving process, creating a picture out of life. Contemplative prayer and active involvement in God's world – these are its two sides. St Paul says that 'all things work together for good for those who love God, who are called according to his purpose'.[2] Contemplation helps me to discern that wise and loving purpose God has for his world; it heightens my awareness and deepens my commitment to it. Active involvement expresses that response to his call and incarnates it in the arena of human struggles and dilemmas. One more tiny piece of the tapestry is created.

MADE FOR JOY AND WOE

That summer of my ordination brought into sharp focus for me the fact that this tapestry we are weaving contains a mixture of colours. There are bright, joyous tones; but there are also sombre hues. The greys, violets and blacks are woven into the tapestry as firmly as the greens, golds and reds. It seems that this darker backdrop is always there; that even (or especially) at times of joy, there is that threat of some crisis, some hint of trouble just over the horizon, if not an actual explosion of pain somewhere else to throw our own celebration into sharp relief. In the musical *Fiddler on the Roof*, the threat of pogroms lies like some lowering cloud over the lives and fortunes of a peasant family. It is during a wedding feast that the violence begins, and the close-knit community faces their impending calamity. In Breughel's painting *The Fall of Icarus*, a world going about its business on a bright summer's day fails to notice the young man plummeting out of the sky to his death.[3] Soldiers played dice, St John tells us, in the shadow of the cross.[4]

On the wall of the room in our home where we do most things other than sleep, hangs a sampler. It is our own, small tapestry. It was made for us as a parting gift on leaving the parish in Northumberland where we had served for five years. It had been an enriching experience to live and work in the far north of England, but it had not been without its share of struggle and pain. There were times when the darkness of those long, winter nights seemed to have taken firm root in my own heart. Spring comes late in those parts. On the sampler, with

great perception, the embroiderers had chosen some words of
William Blake:

> Man was made for Joy and Woe;
> And when this we rightly know,
> Thro' the world we safely go.
> Joy and Woe are woven fine,
> A clothing for the soul divine.[5]

Those are, I have long thought, the most truthful words
England's most truthful poet ever uttered. Perhaps they resonate
for me personally because I find this lesson about joy and woe so
hard to learn. Like most people brought up in the comfort of the
middle class way of life, I instinctively expect misfortune to be
an aberration. It doesn't fit into what I have come to think is
normal and accepted. The dark side of existence, what Blake
calls 'woe', is simply unacceptable and unfair. And so, when it
does surface through a tragic accident, the break up of a close
relationship, illness such as heart disease, cancer or AIDS, we find
it hard to cope. My first discovery that 'joy and woe are woven
fine' is likely to come as a cruel disillusionment. In this, I suspect
we, in our affluent western society, are very far away from our
less affluent forbears, and our less affluent contemporaries in the
Third World, for whom suffering is simply an expected part of
living. They 'rightly know' what we have all but forgotten.

It is astonishing, when I think about it, how easily my
comfortable easy style of Christianity can lose touch with reality.
'The continually stuffed body cannot see secret things,' says the
Amazulu.[6] It cannot even always see what is not secret. Our
Christian story has joy and woe woven into it from beginning
to end. The reality with which I lose touch is not simply the
world around me. It is the very story of Jesus on which my
entire faith rests.

THE MASSACRE OF INNOCENCE

The Christmas story presents us with the most striking – indeed
terrible – images of this. It is a story we tend to hear very

partially. We edit out those aspects of it that disturb our celebrations too radically. We perhaps cope with 'no room at the inn' by making a donation, though Christmas hospitality to the poor or friendless would be a more demanding response. But what has happened to that most frightful New Testament story of all, Matthew's account of the massacre of the innocent children by the tyrannical Herod?

This story[7] belongs squarely to the Christmas cycle, for the deaths of the little children are the direct consequence of the visit by the Magi. Yet it is hardly ever read at Christmas services. Perhaps it is too close to home, this lection, and touches our deepest dreads and fears. If the feast day of the Holy Innocents should fall on the Sunday after Christmas, it is to be transferred to the next day according to the Church of England rules which order the service. The average Sunday congregation will not hear the story at all. Yet here is the truth, that the birth of the saviour, far from bringing peace on earth, takes place against the bloody backdrop of violence and murder on a huge scale. 'The holly bears a berry as red as any blood'. It is a kind of Passiontide in the middle of Christmas.

No matter whether the story has any basis in history or not; no matter that it reflects the archetypal Greek myth of the god Cronus who was so obsessed by the threat that his own children might one day be more powerful than he that he swallowed them alive. The fact is that the Christmas story offers us images that are only too familiar from our television screens: tyranny, oppression, bloodshed and innocent suffering. But we cannot bear this cruelty during the season of merriment and goodwill. We want to believe that the world is not really like this. So we suppress it, and deny the Christmas truth that 'joy and woe are woven fine'. We 'cannot bear very much reality',[8] said T. S. Eliot, least of all, it seems, when it might spoil our fun.

On the tapestry, I see in the cross the massacre of innocence. The woe is faithfully woven into this icon of my life and the world's. There is no pretending that things are other than they really are. What did the weavers think about as they worked on the tortured figure, creating him limb by limb? Did they think about joy and woe as they pondered this slab of grey amid the sea of green and gold? Did they talk to one another about the complex intersections of creative and destructive forces in life as they wove this miracle? For me, these questions will not go away. As I look at the tapestry, as I read the Bible, as I reflect on human history and that tiny trace within it that is my own life, Blake's words ring more true than ever: 'Joy and woe are woven fine'.

Carole King's song *Tapestry* is in my mind as I write. Like Blake, she sees life as a work of art that is painstakingly put together, in her words, a 'wondrous woven magic'. To begin with, the colours are radiant, happy: blue and gold – the colours of childhood, perhaps, for many of us that time of endless sunny days when we had no notion that the world was anything other than a great playground. But the song rapidly leaves that idyll behind as the tapestry is unveiled, and an ominous figure appears, 'gray and ghostly', to cast a shadow over a life once so bright and colourful. To the singer he has come to take her back, remove her from her glorious, multi-coloured world. He elicits dread. All 'wondrous woven magic' has a dark side.[9]

And that is my great fear, as the rollers turn, and what is to come begins to be unveiled. My fear is that the 'rich and royal hue' with which my life began, full of possibility and promise, will end in darkness and gloom. There is something unutterably bleak about the end of that song; yet I have known people for whom life is as bleak as that, who have ended their existence with that irrevocable act of despair, suicide. I think, as I write, of a young woman, one of the most alive people I have known, who took her own life shortly after giving birth to her child. Perhaps in most of us, despair, the figure in black, is kept at bay by very fragile defences. Perhaps this fatal choice not to be could break through in any of us without warning one day, and overwhelm us. Like Mozart, called upon by the mysterious hooded visitant to commission a Requiem, I could easily come to believe that it must be for myself.

Therefore I need faith to see, when times are dark, that

> Under every grief and pine
> Runs a joy with silken twine.[10]

Like Abraham it is often a matter of hoping against hope in a universe that seems at best to be indifferent and, more usually, downright hostile. Yet hope, it seems to me, is born out of hopelessness and despair, those bleak places in life where there is nothing left for us to do *but* to hope. I have needed to learn the hard way that Christianity does not offer to solve my problems, or provide me with crutches with which to negotiate, and if possible survive, this life. What it offers is courage to walk the human road, and to make something worthwhile of the journey. It offers me the tools to turn necessity into art.

DAYS ARE WHERE WE LIVE

I come back to the making of the tapestry at Felletin. I said that at no time during the weaving was the tapestry seen as a whole, only the part being worked on at the time. Yet it was woven as a single piece, a seamless robe.

Here too I find a satisfying image to think about. My life is warp and weft: what is given and what I do with that givenness. It is a single piece, woven as a whole. It holds together threads of many colours for it is a tale of joy and woe. Yet like the tapestry-maker, I can only see the part of my life I am working on at the moment, and maybe, what has recently passed through time's loom. I see what is exposed now. I cannot see the whole, just yet; only a few fragments of colour and shape to hint – no more – at what that whole might look like. I glimpse patterns, an interweaving of motifs, a development. Memory partially fills out the picture of what has been, and informs what now is. But I can never see my story in totality. Ahead lies unwoven warp wrapped around the future's roller. Everything is partial, incomplete, unfinished. I live in the belief that somehow I am creating a picture. I trust that out of this warp and weft is emerging a work of art: my life. I must hold on to the conviction that these fragmentary patterns and shapes that for the time being look perplexing will, when the entire tapestry is unrolled, build up into a coherent, even beautiful, achievement.

The word in my mind as I write this is 'today'. What is unfolded, what I see of my life, are its todays.

> What are days for?
> Days are where we live.
> They come, they wake us
> Time and time over.
> They are to be happy in:
> Where can we live but days?[11]

Put theologically, today is where I am called to love and serve God. The Letter to the Hebrews devotes two whole chapters to expounding that *Venite* warning: 'Today, if you hear his voice, do not harden your hearts.'[12] The here and now is the place in which life happens and God comes to meet me. I easily dwell on the past, any memory of the picture completed thus far, wrapped around one roller; or daydream about the future, the empty warp wrapped around the other. I believe God wants me instead to focus on the weaving that needs to be done on the exposed part of my life today. Indeed, perhaps the extent to which I am truly alive as a human being is measured by my readiness to say 'yes' to life in the present. When Sydney Smith advised, as a help in depression, lighting big fires in every room, and 'taking short views of human life, not further than dinner or tea',[13] I think he was saying much the same thing. The eighteenth century spiritual writer Jean Pierre de Caussade spoke about 'the sacrament of the present moment'.[14] 'Do not worry about tomorrow',[15] says Jesus in the Sermon on the Mount. There is that which can safely be left to God for the time being. My task is to attend to today.

So living, like tapestry making, is an enormous act of faith. Jung was fond of quoting Kierkegaard's saying that life has to be lived forwards and understood backwards.[16] I am too close to it for the time being to see it for what it is. It is all foreground: the swirls of colour, the hints of shape, do not as yet cohere. The joy and the woe are woven fine, but make little sense in relation to each other. That is how it must be until I can, so to speak, step back and see the finished picture, take in the perspective, grasp the relationship between the parts and the whole.

Faith tells me that there must come this point of integration; this time of 'knowing even as I am known', as St Paul puts it.[17] If my life has any meaning, then I dare to believe that one day, I shall be shown what it is. The 'unveiling' is what the weaving of my life is all for. But in what is unveiled, I hope to see what I see at the centre of the great tapestry in Coventry Cathedral. For there, amid the colours both of joy and woe, emerging glorious out of the myriad threads of warp and weft, I see the majestic figure of Christ. I learn the only thing that ultimately matters: that, recognised or not, it is Christ who is there, God-with-us, his incarnate and risen life forever woven fine into ours.

And insofar as I glimpse him now, I begin to celebrate this mystery of the presence of God. I learn to 'greet him the days that I meet him'. And when more than a meeting is offered, some insight perhaps, some new glimpse of truth, well then I 'bless when I understand.'[18]

6

COAT OF MANY COLOURS

BEHIND the tapestry is a wall. Few people have ever seen it. It would be the sheerest, starkest of walls. If you go outside the Cathedral and look up at the tapestry wall, the 'east' end of the Cathedral, you get some idea of how sheer and stark it must be. But now, that bleak expanse of concrete has been covered with the 'wondrous, woven magic' Carole King sings about. It is a coat of many colours,[1] like a 'clothing for the soul divine'. The wall glows. It has come alive.

The colour that immediately strikes you on first approaching the tapestry is its greenness. To be sure, there are 900 different colours altogether, we are told. But it is the green background that you remember. It is 'a nature green, very full and rich, and very pure, neither yellowy nor blueish'.[2] It penetrates the entire Cathedral. And when you have taken in the golds, the violets, the greys, the reds, you come back to that pervasive green which is the background against which all the other colours have to be 'read'.

I pause here, and wonder why the green background is so important, why there is so much of it. It is important, certainly. It appears to me to be like the spaces on a page surrounding a poem, or the silence between the words we speak, or the pauses between the notes in music. Without it, without these spaces or voids, there could be no utterance, no music, no speech. You would have words and symbols crowding in upon one another, cancelling out one another's message. What I find in the tapestry's green is a quality of rest (to use another musical analogy) that enables its images to come alive and sing. I need its 'silence' if the symbols are to speak. I need its restfulness if my spirit, as well as being energised by the tapestry, is to find some repose there too.

BENEDICITE

But the green is itself a symbol. Colour symbolism, the psychology of colour, is very complex. Philosophers continue to

argue about whether you and I are seeing the same 'thing' when we use the language of colour: whether my 'green' is in fact your 'red', and what difference that makes to the way we see the world. But it is generally agreed that colours send coded messages, often subliminally: the clothes I wear, for instance, or choice of colour-scheme in the decoration of my home. No doubt the choice of green as the prevailing colour of the tapestry was suggested primarily by architectural and artistic considerations. Nevertheless, the colour carries meanings of its own that are worth pondering in our meditation.

Like all colours, green stands for many things. 'Greenhorn', 'green-eyed monster' are two of its less attractive connotations. But ask most people what the colour green suggests to them and they will talk about nature, growth, springtime, conservation or the environment. Because of its naturalness, green is an overwhelmingly positive colour. Its choice as the 'go' signal on roads and railways across the world can hardly have been arbitrary. As I grow older, this colour means more and more to me – perhaps out of a nostalgic longing for an ever-receding youth, perhaps in the hope of experiencing 'green old age'; or, I like to think, because as I journey through life to begin to find myself, I sense more and more that I am part of a greater organism, something profoundly alive that brought me forth, whose life nourishes me, sustains me, and to which one day I shall return.

The green of the tapestry speaks to me, then, of the unity of all things and of my part in that unity. It speaks of the story of creation, of a God who 'saw everything that he had made, and indeed, it was very good';[3] of an Eden in which everything was ordered and right; where, because human beings lived in perfect intimacy with God, they also lived in perfect intimacy with plants, animals and the earth. In that story of primeval goodness, I catch William Blake's ecstatic vision:

To see a world in a grain of sand
And a heaven in a wild flower,
Hold infinity on the palm of your hand
And eternity in an hour.[4]

It is a world of total rightness and integration, each part reflecting the glory of the whole, enjoying a God-intended harmonious relationship with every other part: 'perfect diapason',[5] Milton called it.

So this green points me to creation. It makes me think of the aeons it took for green things to cover the barren rock of this planet, just as the green tapestry covers the bare wall of the Cathedral. I ponder the mystery of evolution, of this world constantly in the making, and of Christ through whom all things were made, enthroned amidst this teeming universe of life. The tapestry proclaims him as both Lord of creation and its firstborn: the Christ who is forever bringing to birth, calling cosmos out of chaos, making all things new. Of all this, the tapestry is a marvellous celebration, a Benedicite in cloth summoning all the works of the Lord to praise him and magnify him for ever.

The Benedicite is a magnificent song of creation. One of its most endearing features is the loving attention it pays to the least of creation as well as the greatest. It moves naturally from the splendour of sun, moon and stars to the intimate beauty of dew and frost; from the spectacular displays of lightning and cloud to the ordinary rhythms of winter and summer, night and day; from the grandiose mountains and seas, to the more modest wells. It recognises that God is blessed by all the 'green things upon the earth'. It ends, significantly, with the 'holy and humble at heart' as if to say not only that the spectacle of creation ought to make us humble, but that it is precisely in what is humble and of little account that glory is so often to be found. 'Lift up the stone and you shall find me; cleave the wood and I shall be there. Whoever wonders shall reign',[6] says an old mystic text, reflecting this central insight of the Bible that what is least, often turns out to be the bearer of God himself.

GREEN SPIRITUALITY

I contemplate the tapestry's greenness, and am made to think, not only of the rain forests, but also of the blades of grass in my back garden; not only of Dante's love that moves the sun and the stars, but also of the God who comes 'in the little things' as Evelyn Underhill put it. It is a healing, integrating colour, drawing me back into communion with the created world. Peter Matthiessen, for example, writes with great feeling about a trek through the Himalayas. The ostensible goal of his long and difficult pilgrimage was to catch sight of the rarely glimpsed snow leopard. Despite his failure to see it, the journey became for him a metaphor of his human and spiritual quest. He movingly recaptures his sense of oneness with the world both of the spectacular and the ordinary:

> I grow into these mountains like a moss. I am bewitched. The blinding snow peaks and the clarion air, the sound of earth and heaven in the silence, the requiem birds, the mythic beasts, the flags, great horns, and old carved stones, the rough-hewn Tartars in their braids and homespun boots, the silver ice in the Black River . . . Also I love the common miracle – the murmur of my friends at evening, the clay fires of smudgy juniper, the coarse dull food, the hardship and simplicity, the contentment of doing one thing at a time . . . In another life – this isn't what I know but how I feel – these mountains were my home; there is a rising of forgotten knowledge like a spring from hidden aquifers under the earth. To glimpse one's own true nature is a kind of homecoming.[7]

How far we have moved away from this oneness with creation is only now becoming apparent on a wide scale, although William Blake warned of it nearly 200 years ago as he watched the Industrial Revolution blacken England's 'green and pleasant land'. In our own time, the colour green has come to represent the need to recover our reverence for life, our respect for the fragile ecosystem of this planet that is the home we share with the myriad other species of living things. And insofar as dealing with industrial pollution, the greenhouse effect, and the despoiling of the rain forests is something human beings can only effectively do together, green has become a colour with a political dimension too. It has become the colour of protest against the dehumanising tyranny of technology.

In 1988, we in Coventry collaborated with the Worldwide Fund for Nature in preparing a harvest festival liturgy that would take up these concerns and give them concrete expression. It was all too easy, we felt, for harvest to be an affair of corn dollies and coxes on the altar: beautiful and apposite in its way, but, especially in cities, liable to collapse into little more than an exercise in nostalgia, feeding our longings for a rural idyll that probably never existed. We wanted, in a Cathedral of reconciliation, to express our longing and prayer that humanity might become reconciled to the natural order in a new way. For me, that morning, the tapestry's green seemed more vivid than ever. It seemed silently to rebuke humankind for our relentless soiling of creation, our poisoning of the wellsprings from which we draw our very life. We sang what we called a *Benedicite Lament*:

> Mountains and hills, plants and trees,
> Rivers and oceans, whales and fishes,
> Birds, beasts and cattle,
> Cry aloud to the Lord,
> Save us from destruction
> To praise and magnify you for ever.
> Save us! Save us! Save us![8]

In an act of penitence we prayed:

> Our brothers and sisters of the creation, the mighty trees, the broad oceans, the air, the earth, the creatures of creation; forgive us and reconcile us to you . . . Draw us out to be again a part of all creation, that we may praise and magnify our Lord forever.

On that occasion, liturgy joined art in protesting against our exploitation of the world and its resources. I realised in a new way how the tapestry's greenness calls me to a life of integration and wholeness, a 'creation spirituality'. These insights are not new. You find such a 'green' spirituality in many places and times, for instance among the Indian peoples of North America, or in the Celtic form of Christianity that came to us from Ireland via Iona and Lindisfarne. You find it in the medieval mystical writers such as Hildegard of Bingen and Mother Julian of Norwich.

What marks it out? Such things as its earthiness, its femininity, its feeling for nature and the natural rhythms of night and day, the phases of the moon and the cycle of the seasons. William Blake sees 'a world in a grain of sand and a heaven in a wild flower'.[9] Mother Julian of Norwich holds a tiny hazel nut in the palm of her hand and meditates that 'it is all that is made . . . it lasteth, and ever shall for that God loveth it'.[10] I am put in my place. That reverence for life or, in her words, treating all living things with courtesy because that is how God treats me, is a rebuke to the cavalier way I ignore or, worse, violate the beauty and integrity of even the lowliest forms of life.

I find the same insight in Celtic writing. Such simple acts as laying a fire, milking a cow, or getting dressed in the morning become the occasions for homely, intimate rituals and prayers, signalling that all of life is the gift of God. Celtic art makes the same point visually: in those infinitely varied patterns beloved by the writers of the Book of Kells or the Lindisfarne Gospels, I see the Celtic celebration of the connectedness of everything, the interwovenness (to go back to the tapestry metaphor) of the human, animal, vegetable and inanimate creation; the interwovenness of the whole of creation and the life of God himself. And this, too, is the theme running through the spirituality of the native American peoples, with their veneration of the land of their ancestors as the inalienable gift of the Great Spirit, with all that the land supports being suffused with the Spirit's life-giving presence:

> I wonder if the ground has anything to say? . . . The ground says, it is the Great Spirit that placed me here . . . The ground, water, grass say, the Great Spirit has given us our names. We have these names and hold

these names. The ground says, the Great Spirit has placed me here to produce all that grows on me, trees and fruit. The same way the ground says, it was from me man was made. The Great Spirit, in placing men on the earth, desired them to take good care of the ground and do each other no harm.[10]

This kind of writing, to me, imbues creation with a sacramental, almost eucharistic quality, so strong is its grasp of the insight that the Spirit of God breathes through the natural world. We badly need to recover this joy in all that God has made, this childlike instinct for a world in which God is alive and active and always at work.

TOUCHING THE EARTH

As a child of London, loving that city yet, because of it, a stranger to the real countryside, I am a latecomer to this earth-centredness. It is not enough to say, as a theological affirmation, that 'creation spirituality' is simply the consequence of the doctrines of creation and incarnation. I had, I think, always believed that. What I needed to do was to feel it. This was one of the gifts to me of living for five years in Northumberland. There, in England's remotest county, I felt exposed to nature in a way I have never felt anywhere else. I loved the green, lonely, hump-backed Cheviot Hills, where I would walk for miles with only the larks and the grouse for company. I loved the coast, when a northeasterly gale was blowing, and I would sit for hours on the rocks near the skeleton of Dunstanburgh Castle, watching the North Sea vent its wrath on the shore, feeling myself totally involved with the elemental forces let loose all around me. I felt connected, energised. I attempted to express this sense of exposure in a poem I called Northern Saints:

You look in vain for some
Shelter at our northern
Shrines. That is their

Forbidding glory. These are
Bleak places without
Trees. Nothing much
Grows here except
Holiness. They have been
Hospitable only to
God and to prayer. Yet a

Presence has touched the
Uncurious soil. Its
Resonances linger on,
Bricked up beneath
Jarrow's forlorn pavements,
Battered by the
East wind's assault on
Lindisfarne, or
Congealed in the hardened
Veins of men pitted against
Northumberland. You might be

Tempted to say that these shrines are
God-forsaken, for he has been
This way once and passed on. Yet their very
Emptiness is religious. There is
No hiding here, no
Evading his absence, no
Obscuring comfort to help you
Pretend. Naked the
Sullen land confronts the
Souring sky, and the
Sharp line of their
Meeting is the etched-out
Truth of the north, that in such
Cruel juxtaposition is the
Holiness that forges
Saints. Religion should be as
Exposed as this.

Now that I live once more in a city, a long way from the sea and the fells I love, I need to find other ways of celebrating this 'connectedness', this green insight that I am of the earth, and the earth is God's gift to me. My own way of doing this has been to discover the hobbies of bread and wine making. Both are satisfying in themselves: collecting the raw materials – flour in bulk from an old mill in Warwickshire, fruits, flowers and berries from the hedgerows of an abandoned railway line that becomes an amazingly beautiful place each spring and autumn; the use of my hands in making up the dough or preparing the must; the waiting while the yeast works its miracle of transformation, and sharing with others the enjoyment of the finished product: bread and wine, fruit of the earth, the work of my human hands. I find in these homely activities that my suburban existence is given a redeeming quality. I feel connected once more, part of the earth. And when the bread I bake is for use at the Cathedral eucharist, I feel more than ever this connection between spirituality and the world of living, growing things. It reinforces faith in this 'God of earth and altar'.

This discovery and making contact with the earth – whether in the garden, or through sport and physical exercise, or through bird-watching or collecting rocks and minerals – is a sign of something much deeper. It is more than 'nature mysticism' and more than a middle class, romantic flirtation with wholefoods and recycled paper. It is, or should be, a sign of ecological seriousness. This kind of spirituality demands that we repent, as a race, of the selfish damage we inflict upon the environment; and it calls us to make the practical, political decisions that alone can rescue the world from the deep crisis into which we have plunged it. It requires that we take seriously the Old Testament claim that we are stewards of creation, priests to it, loving and reverencing it, working and caressing it as a breadmaker works the dough.

The Sap Rising

It is easy, when confronted almost daily with ecological horror stories, to lose hope. Yet there are signs of hope. I came across one in London on a recent visit when, in the vicinity of Euston Station, I looked for somewhere to eat. Behind a glass and concrete office block, and sheltered by it from the roar of traffic, I found a peaceful pedestrianised square. New housing had been built on three sides, front doors opening directly onto a lovingly landscaped oasis of grass, trees and shrubs. On the fourth side of the square was a pub. Here, I felt, the wilderness had blossomed. Not only was nature cherished here, but human community as well. Many such stories can be told from the bleakest, most unpromising of contexts. The green of the tapestry helps me not to lose heart, to keep hoping. It signals new beginnings, paradise restored.

Lawrence Binyon, the First World War poet, is most famous for his lines *For the Fallen*: 'They shall grow not old, as we that are left grow old'. Less well-known is a fine poem, in a similarly elegiac mood, that celebrates the autumn. To him, the autumn bonfire, the burning of leaves and the year's dead wood is a symbol of what has been lost for ever: lost youth, lost innocence, the lost certainties of a world that died for ever in 1914.

> Now is the time for stripping the spirit bare,
> Time for the burning of days ended and done,
> Idle solace of things that have gone before:
> Rootless hopes and fruitless desire are there;
> Let them go to the fire, with never a look behind.
> The world that was ours is a world that is ours no more.

It is a poem that reeks of death, decay and destruction. But it is not a hopeless, despairing piece of writing. Its last stanza looks beyond the mists and frosts to the new growth on the other side of winter.

> They will come again, the leaf and the flower, to arise
> From squalor of rottenness into the old splendour,
> And magical scents to a wondering memory bring;
> The same glory, to shine upon different eyes.
> Earth cares for her own ruins, naught for ours.
> Nothing is certain, only the certain spring.[12]

It is a fact of autumn that as the leaves fall, the sap is already rising. I need to remember that when I am tempted, as I often am, to despair at what we are doing to our planet. Binyon's words may seem to be shouting into the wind. But they reflect the conviction, at the heart of the gospel, that 'paradise restored' is more than a day dream. The Christian hope is for 'a new heaven and a new earth'.[13] It is depicted in profoundly ecological terms. There is the pure river of the water of life; there are trees bearing fruit; pollution, sickness and death are things of the past.

At the heart of Coventry's tapestry, enthroned amidst the green, is the risen Christ who says, 'Behold, I make all things new'. There is, faith tells me, a certain spring for our world, a recovery of Eden. 'Now the green blade riseth from the buried grain', runs the carol. I take heart. In the green, I recognise Easter.

7

BEAUTY AND THE BANDS

THE COLOUR green, I have suggested, links me to the rest of creation. God's world is one, and I am called to live as part of that one world, celebrating the God-givenness of its life. What I am feeling after is a connected life – a way of living that is 'part of' rather than 'apart from'. 'No man is an island entire of itself', says John Donne; and if I am indeed part of the main, 'involved in mankind' as he says, then I am just as surely involved in all living things, all creation. The bell that tolls for them tolls for me.

How do I make this feeling conscious? How do I give shape to this sense that, in Origen's words,

> You yourself are even another little world and have within you the sun and the moon and also the stars?[1]

THE LIGAMENTS OF LIFE

Superimposed on the green of the tapestry are lines of gold: a gold aureole surrounding the figure of Christ in the centre, and horizontal and vertical bands cutting across the sward of green to the tapestry's edge. Graham Sutherland tells us[2] that these bands of gold, so to speak, 'hold' the picture in place, binding it together and to the building, preventing the constituent parts – Christ, the four living creatures, St Michael and the devil – from appearing to float in a sea of green. Artistically, they give the tapestry its shape, its coherence. The whole composition, as we say, 'hangs together'.

In this, I see an image of God at work in creation and in human life. I see the bands of gold as introducing order and pattern into that sea of green. They give form and structure to what, otherwise, would appear without form. And that is the Bible's primary picture of the act of creation: bringing order out of what was, at the beginning of time, 'tohu wa vohu', a 'formless void'.[3] The first chapter of Genesis provides a marvellous hymnic unfolding of this ordering process as, day by day, light is separated from darkness, and dry land from the waters; the species of plant and animal life are distinguished from one another, 'each according to its kind'; and finally, human beings are created. The Great Chain of Being, as the medieval theologians called the hierarchy of creation, is complete. Out of chaos has been born cosmos.

Throughout the Bible, this story of creation is appealed to as a model of the ordered human life, the life that has shape and pattern, that is not just a formless void. The legendary wisdom of King Solomon, for instance, is connected with his study of the natural world: 'He would speak of trees, from the cedar that is in Lebanon to the hyssop that grows in the wall; he would speak of animals, and birds, and reptiles, and fish. People came from all the nations to hear the wisdom of Solomon; they came from all the kings of the earth who had heard of his wisdom'.[4] Throughout the wisdom literature of the Old Testament, creation is held up as an icon of orderliness, pattern and meaning. 'Go to the ant, you lazybones; consider its ways and be wise'.[5] The message is plain: if you would have insight, judgement, discernment (which is the meaning of wisdom), take a leaf out of creation's book and order your life accordingly. Not to do that is to remain in chaos, in a formless, shapeless existence that falls far short of what the Old Testament means by living. The psalmist's picture of that condition is the chaff which the wind drives away.[6]

In the New Testament, it is the same. Early in St Mark's gospel, Jesus calms the storm,[7] just as the Spirit of God hovered at the beginning of time over the chaotic waters of the primal ocean and ordered them. Mark intends this to be a picture of what happens when Jesus is given entry into human lives: our storms are stilled, our chaos given order, our voids filled with shape and meaning. For he immediately goes on to tell of the Gerasene demoniac whom no-one could restrain, whose domain was 'among the tombs and on the mountains' – places of dereliction and death.[8] The healing of this man, and his testimony to 'how much Jesus had done for him' is a paradigm, for Mark, of the ordering, life-restoring impact of the kingdom of God coming amongst human beings.

Every Christian has his or her own visual aid of this God who invades life in order to set it right, bring divine order to it, make it new. I mean, of course, baptism. The waters of baptism are meant, at one level, to be like the waters of storm-tossed Genessaret: chaotic, threatening disintegration and death. Into that disorder I am plunged; ritually drowned. In St Paul's words, I am 'buried with Christ in baptism',[9] given up to the forces of destruction. My old life is finished. I am as if I were back at the beginning of Genesis 1, 'without form and void', awaiting my new identity, the gift of the Spirit hovering above the water. Only so can God perform his new creation, raise me up with Christ to the new life of Easter. Only so do the waters of death become transformed into the life-giving womb waters of new birth. (How can baptism be an effective way of dramatising this good news, unless it is with lots of water, and preferably by immersion?)

This divine ordering of life is the purpose of religion. The word *religio* literally appears to mean 'tying back' or attachment, as in *ligature, ligament*. Religion 'ties me back' to God, just as the golden bands on the tapestry are the ligaments tying the images together, binding them around Christ who is the centre of everything. And in this binding and bonding, just as on the tapestry, patterns emerge, order appears. John Calvin likens the ordering impact of the word of God to putting on spectacles.[10] The chaotic, formless images condense into shapes, as walking trees became human beings to the blind man Jesus healed.[11] Things come into focus. I can see. The tapestry's green is a marvellous colour. But it needs the bands of gold to set it off in its true splendour. The mystery of life, the profound mystery of myself, needs the shaping and structuring presence of religious faith if I am to appreciate it for what it is. I need stability if I am to grow as a human being and as a child of God. I need a symmetry of the spirit.

STABILITY

[We have] at the back of our minds . . . a forgotten
blaze or burst of astonishment at our own existence.
The object of the artistic and spiritual life is to dig for
this submerged sunrise of wonder.[12]

In our human journey, stability is already given to us in many
ways: the family relationships we are born into; the places where
they are largely lived out, our homes; the natural rhythms of day
and night, the seasons, the turning of weeks and years that
define our path through life and mark out times for work, play
and rest. The tragedy of those without home, family or work is
partly a lack of precisely this fundamental, God-given stability,
this shaping and patterning that is so basic to human life.

Next to the north wall of Coventry Cathedral are some
ancient stumps of stone, rather like fossilised tree-trunks. They
turn out to be the remains of the first cathedral to be built on
that site by Leofric and Godiva in 1043. At the other end of the
street, there are more. If ever a great medieval building was
successfully razed to the ground by the religious crises of the
16th century, this one was: on the surface, hardly anything is to
be seen. But beneath the Georgian buildings that now overlay
the site, there will be significant relics of the nave walls, and
further down still, the foundations.

These remains, disjointed on the surface, but embedded into
the ground I walk on, recall me to my roots. This abbey church
was home to a community of monks who followed the
Benedictine way. This religious ideal was for shape and stability
in all of life. Benedict's vision of an ordered, balanced life
bequeathed to the world one of the greatest of religious classics,
his incomparable *Rule*. His story itself is an illustration of the
issues we are exploring in this chapter. The world into which he
was born, in northern Italy, was a highly unstable, chaotic one.
Europe was in pieces following the fall of the Roman empire; no
power had yet arisen to fill the vacuum the Caesars had left
behind. It was in this situation of political and cultural disarray
that Benedict turned away from the solitary life and began to

establish monasteries, groups of monks discovering community in a fragmented world, committed by his *Rule*, to a common life of disciplined work, study and prayer.

The *Rule* is a modest, workmanlike document – 'this least of rules,' he calls it.[13] It sets out to be no more than a guide to the Christian life as it is lived in community, written for beginners rather than experts, for lay people rather than clergy. Its aim is to model 'a school of the Lord's service'. In it, Benedict claims to have written 'nothing that is harsh or rigorous'.[14] Rather, he is attempting to give shape to the common life that is based on one supreme premise – the grace of God in Christ, and the living out of the life of gratitude that is our response to this gospel fact.

Stability, the ordered life, says Benedict, rests on three priorities: prayer, work and study. Roughly speaking, the monks were required to divide their time equally between the three. *Prayer*, because the saying of the divine office, the Opus Dei or 'work of God', is making conscious and articulate our response to God's love, and the offering of our lives to him. *Work*, because to serve God demands that we serve one another, maintaining the community in its day to day life, meeting the needs of the poor and, in these ways, honouring the God-given abilities that lie in our human hands. *Study*, because the exploration of Scripture and the writings of wise and holy men and women deepens our understanding of faith and love, and keeps alive our sense of wonder at the mystery of grace.

Such a rule of life is what I need to find for myself if my life is to achieve some shape, some order. Those three Benedictine pillars will be good places to start. I may need to broaden the concepts somewhat. *Prayer* will include any activity that deepens my response to God and articulates my 'yes' to life: meditation, contemplation, active imagination, dream work, silence, as well as formal public worship. *Work* will not be restricted merely to paid employment or domestic chores, but will include the offering of my time and talents as I involve myself in the life of church and world, and in the lives of others. *Study* will mean more than exploring books, or even the Book. It will include everything that helps me pay attention to what matters in life, feeds me and helps me to grow; the arts, for instance, or spiritual direction; psychotherapy perhaps, and other ways to self-awareness and maturity. And I will need very probably to add to these: *leisure*, for example, and the cultivation of my *intimate relationships*.

ASCETIC AND AESTHETIC

The prophet Zechariah writes of 'the beauty and the bands'.[15] The 'beauty' I can warm to: the 'high' experiences, the liturgy (on good days), meeting Christ in my fellow travellers. The 'bands' I find much harder: the discipline of Christian living, bothering enough not to walk by on the other side, Lent. Yet the tapestry calls me back to see that these are two sides of the same coin. You cannot have 'beauty' without 'bands'. If it seems that way, then it is an illusion. The process of creation is an act of divine discipline on a cosmic scale: God holding himself back, ordering and channelling his energies, giving shape to the formless void. The powerful myths we find in all cultures of the primordial struggle between the god and the monsters of the deep tell us that this orderliness was hard-won. It had to be fought for. In my own life, too, there are monsters to be battled with: the disordered parts of my being, the demons within. To fight against evil was why monks chose the religious life, the enclosure of the monastery. Those fossilised relics from Coventry's first cathedral remind me of this. It was why St Cuthbert spent his closing years alone on the bleak island of Inner Farne.[16] It is why I need a discipline to live by, why I need bands as well as beauty.

The disciplined slog of the artist is a good metaphor for this creative process. Sutherland's tapestry was ten years in the making. During those years, no less than 155 studies, three cartoons and innumerable sketches were made by the artist elaborating, refining and perfecting his initial vision.[17] One tenth inspiration, nine tenths perspiration is probably on the generous side. R. S. Thomas has a poem that encapsulates it. It is a conversation between two poets about how poetry comes to be written.

'Listen, now, verse should be as natural
As the small tuber that feeds on muck
And grows slowly from obtuse soil
To the white flower of immortal beauty.'

'Natural, hell! What was it Chaucer
Said once about the long toil
That goes like blood to the poem's making?
Leave it to nature and the verse sprawls,
Limp as bindweed, if it break at all
Life's iron crust. Man, you must sweat
And rhyme your guts taut, if you'd build
Your verse a ladder.'

'You speak as though
No sunlight ever surprised the mind
Groping on its cloudy path.'

'Sunlight's a thing that needs a window
Before it enters a dark room.
Windows don't happen.'[18]

This offers me new insight on the idea I have already played with, that God wants me to be the artist of my own developing life. I find it to be an increasingly thought-provoking metaphor. If Thomas is right, if Sutherland is right, then my life will not be something that will simply 'happen' – not, at any rate, if I look for shape in it, orderliness, the imprint of God's image and likeness. There is, there has to be, a *discipline* in it, just as there is a discipline implied in the story of how God fashioned the world, just as there is a discipline spelled out in Benedict's vision of wholeness in which human lives become ever *more* human because ever more stable, more ordered, more God-like.

The traditional word for this discipline is *ascesis*. Literally, this frightening-sounding concept simply means 'training', the kind of training an athlete undergoes if he or she is to be in top form for the race. As I read the lives of writers, artists and composers down the ages, I realise that there has to be an 'ascetic' of art no less than an 'aesthetic': bands of discipline as well as beauty of conception. And as I think of my own life in this way, I realise that here too an 'ascetic' of life is asked of me as well as an 'aesthetic'. Only in that way will it be fit for God's service.

It is a favourite image of St Paul,[19] this metaphor of spiritual fitness. 'Athletes exercise self-control in all things', he says; 'so I do not run aimlessly'. To contend for the prize is, literally, to *agonise*. That will be painful, difficult and hard. Often, I am deflected from that upward call, despite knowing in my heart of hearts that nothing can be more worthwhile. Often, I settle for a comfortable, easy-going Christianity that demands nothing except the lipservice of its familiar, reassuring rituals. I am better, I think, at the holiness of beauty, than the beauty of holiness.

UNHEROIC SANCTITY

Perhaps it is misleading to press the analogy of the artist or the athlete too far. Heroic endeavour of any kind can have a debilitating, depressing effect on people who, like me, are unheroic by temperament. Heroic sanctity can be the most depressing of all to measure yourself up against. I need a way of being that can genuinely be God-given, yet somehow modest, unassuming, a kind of 'heaven in ordinary' as George Herbert calls it,[20] an ascetic that is also an aesthetic of the everyday.

So I look around the ordinariness of daily life for opportunities to develop this unheroic sanctity. A hymn speaks about 'the trivial round, the common task': the theatres of our workshops, our kitchens, our office desks where we learn to practise the presence of God; and most of all, of course, in the daily criss-crossing of our lives with one another as colleagues, neighbours, members of families, and friends. 'Holiness', said Pusey, 'consists not in doing uncommon things, but in doing common things in an uncommon way'. As I grow older, I become, I want to think, less ambitious about doing (and being seen to do) uncommon, heroic things for God (not to mention myself). And I learn more and more the gentle, earthy Old Testament wisdom that holiness is about pennies as well as pounds, kitchen cleanliness as well as temple ritual, baskets of fruit and a few ears of corn that are as pleasing to God as cities and kingdoms hewn down and rebuilt. Here, I discover, is where the ligaments of life are, where I am a learner in the school of God where the curriculum consists of but a single subject: to do justly, and to love mercy, and to walk humbly with him.

But the ligaments on the tapestry are golden. I always come back to that: not black and forbidding, not red and bloodstained, but golden. This way of living, they seem to say, is bright with promise. There is joy as well as duty, pleasure and not pain. They glow with the same radiance that surrounds Christ in glory, for they are the key to living the transfigured life, where simple everyday things take on a beauty of their own. 'Do not chain yourself with chains of iron,' says Benedict; 'rather, let Christ be the chain that binds you.' At the end of the golden string, says Blake, we find the gate of heaven.[21]

That is the secret of the connected life. That is how I begin to unearth that 'forgotten blaze', that 'submerged sunrise of wonder'. Perhaps the golden bands on the tapestry are bands of fire, signs of the Pentecostal blaze that the Dove at its apex wants to bring to our lives. I love the story told by the desert fathers that illustrates how discipline is related to ecstasy, ascetic to aesthetic, law to love:

> Abbot Lot came to Abbot Joseph and said, 'Father, according as I am able, I sing a few psalms, and I pray a little, and my fasting is little, and my prayers, and silent meditations; and as far as lies in my power I cleanse my thoughts. What more can I do?' Then the old man stood up, and stretched out his hands towards heaven, and his fingers became like ten lamps of fire. He said: 'Why not be totally changed into fire?'[22]

There is beauty in the bands.

Part Two

CLOSER IN

'What does the Tapestry mean?' I asked. 'What does it mean to you?'

Andrew Harvey, *A Journey in Ladakh*

8

THE HIGH WINDOW:
THE LIGHT AND THE DOVE

SKY, THOU SEEST ME!

THE TAPESTRY is immense. I find that its sheer size, however overwhelming, somehow evokes trust and reassurance. John Dunne writes of walking amongst the giant redwood trees of California: 'It was very healing to be near them . . . the fatigue of the days dropped from us, and we were small creatures again in a big world made by God.'[1] Mountains, moorlands, the sea evoke similar, creaturely echoes. For me it is the sky that puts me in my place. I have always loved the sound of the word itself – 'sky'; somehow, it evokes in me what Freud called that 'vast, oceanic feeling', something mysterious, primitive, basic. The Slavs would gaze up at it and pray, 'Sky, thou seest me! Sky, thou hearest me!'[2] That is a prayer I can understand. Our Christian story of the Ascension perhaps allows us to pray it once more.

It was when I worked in Wiltshire that this feeling for the sky became conscious. There the sky seems to hang huge and endless over the wide, ancient plains where, since the beginning of time, human beings have wondered at it, and built monuments to it, as at Stonehenge. Then we moved to Northumberland, where the sky is wider still, and lonelier over the bare-backed Cheviots; somehow older, more elemental; often brooding, lowering, intense. Under it, saints like Aidan, Cuthbert and Bede followed Christ and were made holy; and their disciples like Chad, who learnt the faith beneath the Northumbrian sky and brought it to the Midlands where the tapestry now hangs. For me, the sky is one of the joyful mysteries of life.

Beyond the Window

We do not see the sky in the tapestry, unless it is in the indigo of the mandorla surrounding Christ. But at the very top, as if through a window at noon in summer streams in the light. What lies on the other side 'out there' is only hinted at. We do not have to guess, however. The light, pouring in like a liquid, tells of the sun and the sky.

> Rather than words comes the thought of high windows:
> The sun-comprehending glass,
> And beyond it, the deep blue air, that shows
> Nothing, and is nowhere, and is endless.[3]

The high window is an image of the transcendence I talked about at the beginning. Sutherland tells us that the original commission to design the tapestry stated that 'though the form of God himself cannot be depicted, yet the glory of his being must somehow be represented, e.g. Light ('light unapproachable') either above or around the figure of Christ.'[4] The window and the light, together with its unseen source, are a symbol of what cannot be put into words or images. God is 'more than'. He is, as theologians put it, 'wholly other'. He is beyond anything I can contemplate, more mysterious and more wonderful than my feeble imagination can conceive.

Mystery, transcendence: words like these are increasingly important to me as I grow older, and more modest as to the limits of my human capacity to grasp reality. There are more things in heaven and earth, yes and in the depths of my own self, than once I dreamed of. Archbishop Michael Ramsey used to talk about the dignity of creaturehood of which the first virtue was humility. The longest section of St Benedict's *Rule*, which we explored in the last chapter, is about humility. One of the diseases afflicting much religion today is its arrogant lack of humility, its belief that the mystery of God can be packaged in easy words or formulae and purveyed as a marketable commodity. Such a God is too small, and too uninteresting, for he is too knowable. Luther's *Deus Absconditus* is altogether more biblical: 'Truly, thou art a God that hidest thyself.'⁵ The philosopher Wittgenstein warns us: 'Of that whereof we cannot speak, we must remain silent.'⁶ The tapestry is wisely reticent about God. We see only his unapproachable light, the outskirts of his ways. That is an adult, mature unknowing. One of the greatest preachers of Victorian England, the now all but forgotten F. W. Robertson, put it like this:

> The truth is infinite as the firmament above you. In childhood, both seemed near and measurable: but with the years they grow and grow; and seem further off, and further and grander and deeper and vaster, as God himself; till you smile to remember how you thought you could touch the sky, and blush to recollect the proud and self-sufficient way in which you used to talk of knowing or preaching 'The Truth.'⁷

I come back to the image of the high window and light pouring through, entering the dark room of the world's life, of mine. The point about this transcendent God is that he is always piercing the fabric of time and space, pervading the world with his life-giving energy, coming among us as life, light and love. When he comes, there is a profound disturbance. 'O Lord, thou hast searched me out and known me.'⁸ But it is a healing, transforming disturbance. The wound is an act of love and grace. It illuminates. Things begin to glow with a 'borrowed shining' like planets reflecting the light of the sun. I see the ordinary, the everyday, in a new way, like those marvellous interiors of Vermeer where the light from outside makes a miracle of a tiled floor, a woman playing the virginals, or a vase of flowers.

Any number of biblical allusions can be seen in the light and the window. We could see in it the first act of creation, 'Let there be light. And there was light,'⁹ and remember that stunning moment early on in Haydn's Oratorio *The Creation* when, after the shifting, elusive harmonies of the overture representing chaos, the full choir and orchestra suddenly affirm their brilliant C major chord on the word 'light', and the darkness is banished forever. Or we could see in it the incarnation, with St John's wondering proclamation of the true Light that has come into the world, the light that the darkness has not been able to overcome.[10] Or we could see here the baptism of Jesus; or his transfiguration; or his resurrection; or his ascension and enthronement. The point is that in all these stories we have a picture of the divine presence breaking in with the energy of love and grace to make and remake, to know and be known, to open heaven itself and disclose the glory which is our destiny.

And that is a picture of my own life as I should like it to be: turned towards the light like a sunflower, with the sunshine pouring through the window into the bleak house of my being, exposing the dark nooks and crannies, bringing warmth back into cold, damp rooms. And there are windows enough in this interior castle of mine, to borrow Teresa of Avila's striking image, that need flinging open to let in light and air. Some – a few – I know about well enough, and the choice is mine. Others – far more – I know less of, maybe nothing at all. I need the help of others to see where windows need opening. This is the vital function of sacramental confession, spiritual direction and therapy. I need also to listen to my unconscious through my dreams and hear what God is saying to me out of the deep, dark recesses of my soul.

THE CHINKS OF TIME

Sometimes, windows get opened despite ourselves. We are taken by surprise, like the prophet Isaiah in the temple, or Saul of Tarsus on the Damascus Road. There is a shaking of the foundations, a profound turning-round, a seeing things in a radically new way. The consequences can be momentous: politically as well as personally.

In the history of our own times, few individuals can have had a more far-reaching impact on the destiny of millions than Gandhi. At the age of twenty-four, the young lawyer was offered an appointment in South Africa. Not long after arriving, he had the experience that was to change his entire life. Holding a first-class railway ticket, he was roughly pushed out of his

compartment by a Pietermaritzburg guard, and found refuge in a cold, dark waiting room.

> I began to think of my duty. Should I fight for my rights or go back to India, or should I go on to Pretoria? . . . The hardship to which I was subjected was superficial – only a symptom of the deep disease of colour prejudice. I should try, if possible, to root out the disease and suffer hardships in the process . . . So I decided to take the next available train to Pretoria.

Gandhi's practice of non-violence began from that date.'[11]

Most of us can, if we think about it, recall situations and events that, however undramatically, have changed our lives: a chance encounter, a journey, a word or phrase suddenly leaping out of the page, something seen on television. 'A bolt is shot through somewhere in our breast;'[12] a window is opened. I have already described the experience of first seeing the tapestry as a boy. Perhaps another autobiographical story is allowed.

My early experience as a Christian during my teenage and student years was of an evangelical kind. I owe a tremendous amount to those years, and to the friends who nurtured me. But, without realising it, I was becoming more and more trapped in a rigid fundamentalism that, in its insistence on the verbal infallibility of Scripture, was destroying my spiritual life. At the evangelical theological college where I trained prior to ordination, I was told by a tutor to bury myself in the synoptic problem, and not come up until I had solved it to my own satisfaction. For many days I studied the Greek texts of the gospels in parallel. I checked lexica and concordances, and read commentaries. This, for many people, dry-as-dust problem absorbed me. And as I looked at the discrepancies between the four gospels' accounts of Holy Week, and began to see how each writer worked, not as a stenographer but as a creative artist, lovingly painting his own portrait of Jesus, I realised quite suddenly that fundamentalism was a mistake. I began to read the more radical New Testament critics and found that my faith was stimulated. I began to explore the catholic tradition of spirituality and discovered the same. It was a sea-change for me. Windows opened in many rooms of my life; the light flooded in. I was able, under God, to think my own thoughts, to follow where my journey led me, to be myself. I could breathe. I did not solve the synoptic problem; but I solved a far more important problem of my own.

I don't want to make too much of this. It is a very ordinary sort of story. Maturing and growing as a 'human being' is, or ought to be, a lifelong process of opening windows. The seventeenth century poet Edmund Waller, shortly before his death, wrote a poem entitled 'Of the Last Verses in the Book'. It ends in words I find very poignant:

> The soul's dark cottage, batter'd and decay'd,
> Lets in new Light thro' chinks that time has made.
> Stronger by weakness, wiser Men become
> As they draw near to their Eternal home:
> Leaving the Old, both Worlds at once they view,
> That stand upon the threshold of the New.[13]

God, time and circumstance have a way of working that I cannot predict: making chinks, opening windows. The light at the top of the tapestry invites me to place myself in its aura, to bathe in its warmth. 'The only thing wanting is the necessary thing, a great patch of open sky like this. Always try to keep a patch of sky above your life,' the young hero of Proust's *A La Recherche du Temps Perdu* is told at the outset of his monumental journey of self-discovery. 'You have a soul in you of rare quality . . . never let it starve for lack of what it needs.'[14] 'If we walk in the light, as he is in the light', says the great New Testament theologian of light, St John, 'we have fellowship with one another, and the blood of Jesus his Son cleanses us from all sin.'[15]

THE DOVE DESCENDING

There is one more insight the tapestry offers. Right at the apex of the composition, just where the light comes in through the high window, is the figure of a dove. It is one of the tiniest things in the tapestry. Many people don't see it at all. Yet this fragile dove is crucial to everything we have explored in this chapter. For her presence tells me that this wonderful, transcendent light that pours in is more than naked energy, more than the radiance of distant sun or stars. The dove tells me that this light is personal, for she is the judging-yet-saving light of a God in relationship with his creation. The dove comes as God my mother, my lover, my bride; she comes as divine guest looking for a home, and as heavenly messenger bearing news of peace. And she descends upon the head of Christ himself, as in the story of his baptism, to proclaim him as God's beloved Son, the one in whom heaven is opened to us and we see love incarnate.

The dove is a feminine image. Yet the distant, fragile figure remains an image of transcendence: she flies free. She comes to earth without being earthbound. She speaks to me of this 'more than' quality of God that I spoke about earlier. And although she is a feminine image, she comes with all the awesome power of God, just as the Spirit fell as a mighty wind and tongues of fire on the disciples at the first Pentecost. Like the light, she comes to disturb in order that she may caress, to wound so that she may heal. It is hard not to think of T. S. Eliot:

> The dove descending breaks the air
> With flame of incandescent terror
> Of which the tongues declare
> The one discharge from sin and error.
> The only hope, or else despair
> Lies in the choice of pyre or pyre –
> To be redeemed from fire by fire.[16]

Again comes that question posed by the desert fathers: 'why not be totally changed into fire?' If this dove descends upon me, upon our world, might it not be that our life begins to burn without being consumed, like the bush where Moses learned to know God's glory? Might it not be that every patch of soil I walk upon becomes holy ground, as God-filled as the patch of sky over my head?

But the dove also tells me that, in Mother Julian's marvellous phrase, love was his meaning:

> Who then devised the torment? Love.
> Love is the unfamiliar Name
> Behind the hands that wove
> The intolerable shirt of flame,
> Which human power cannot remove.
> We only live, only suspire
> Consumed by either fire or fire.

This is the gift of the high window. From far across the deep blue air beyond floods the light that is life to me. Borne on that sunbeam the dove descends. Because of that window I am searched out and known. That exposure is painful. But there is another knowledge that comes through that window with the light and the dove. I know that I am loved.

9

THE VIOLENCE BENEATH:
THE CRUCIFIXION

THERE IS no light without shadow. The tapestry is honest
about this: 'joy and woe are woven fine'. Corresponding to
the burst of light at the top of the tapestry is a shadow at the
bottom. Opposite the sunshine, there is a darkness; opposite
the fire, ash; opposite the life, a death.

AT THE NADIR

The crucifixion on the tapestry forms the reredos to the Lady
Chapel altar. To that extent, it is something of a separate
composition. There are no gold bands 'tying' it to the figures
above. It seems to stand alone. And yet I find I have to interpret
the lower part of the tapestry in the light of the upper. Wherever
I am, my eye is constantly drawn upwards, as if to say the
tapestry, and the message it conveys, are one.

Seen in this way, the relationship between these two parts
of the tapestry takes on a wealth of meaning. I look at Christ
in glory above; and at once, what is below takes on a
subterranean feeling. The crucifixion takes place beneath the
feet both of Christ and of the man – as if it were already in hell
itself. I am in the underworld, the ashen grey twilight zone.
Sun and moon, in the crucifixion panel, veil their faces. In
contrast to the dove descending, so full of energy and life,
down here the man on the cross is cold with death. No light
penetrates this basement from the high window. It is a God-
forsaken place.

I cannot help seeing here a metaphor of human life. The
crucifixion is a violent act, one of the cruellest forms of
execution men (for surely they were men) have devised. But the
violence on the tapestry is relegated below stairs, so to speak.

The stillness and serenity of Christ in glory seem a different world from the conflict and torment below. There is a poem by Elizabeth Jennings that tells of how, beneath the calm still surface of things, there is a shaking world:

> Under all this
> There is violence.
> The chairs, tables, pictures, paper-weights
> Are all moving, moving.
> You can't see it but they are being carried
> Along with currents and continents.
> We too are carried . . .
> And nothing, nothing is still.[1]

If you live on the San Andreas Fault, you do not need to be told how destructive those subterranean forces are that, without warning, can be unleashed on a world going about its normal, civilised business. In the depths of the tapestry stands the crucifixion, an event that, in St Matthew's account of it, causes the earth to quake and its rocks to be rent.[2] In this shadow, there is violence. At this nadir, at the point furthest away from the light at the zenith, there is agony.

And that is what I mean when I see in this a picture of life. In the 'green' world of living things, nature shows herself to be 'red in tooth and claw', almost unbelievably cruel in the violence that is the cost of evolution. It is one of the 'trials of life'. In the human world of society, there lurk beneath the surface staggering forces of cruelty and destruction, as the names of Auschwitz and Hiroshima, Cambodia and Bosnia have made us only too aware in this century alone. I wrote earlier about the massacre of the innocents in the Christmas story. And the most disconcerting thing of all is to find this same 'shadow', this violent, unredeemed propensity within my own self too. How else can we account for the atrocities otherwise 'decent' men and women were prepared to commit in the name of Nazism? Or 'normal' parents, like you and me, who suddenly 'flip' and batter their babies to death? Or the irrational and unlooked for surge of excitement that we

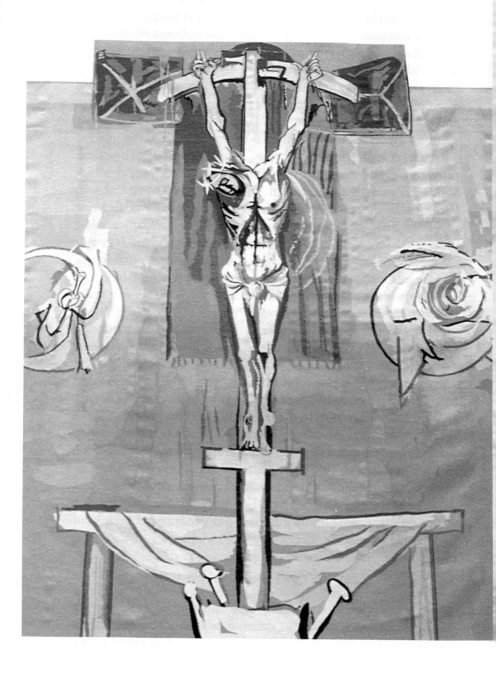

mother's family perished in Auschwitz. Who can understand the meaning of such a hellish place? Perhaps it is the place of non-meaning, a black hole in the tapestry of history. The Jewish novelist Elie Wiesel puts it searchingly:

> 'You won't understand' whispered my father. 'Nobody will understand.' And my mother, in the very beginning, would agree. 'As for me, it is God I do not understand.' To which my father answered, 'And who tells you that God himself understands?'[8]

I look at the crucifixion and I do not understand. Did God understand why cruel men put his Son to death? But in the solitude of his dying, I glimpse one thing. It is that the sufferings and deaths of the many have to be seen in terms of the suffering and death of the one. Alan Bennett, in his film *102 Boulevard Haussmann*, has the novelist Marcel Proust reflect on the slaughter of the First World War:

> The deaths of tens of thousands happening every day is the most insignificant of sensations. One death means more than a thousand. When men are dying like flies, that is what they are dying like.

The point is that men and women do not die in their thousands. They die as individuals, unique, irreplaceable, precious. The crucifixion of Jesus is an image of every death. It is stark, lonely and sad. The light fails. Yet there is nobility too, the offering of a unique, irreplaceable precious life. His life, and mine.

The crucifixion on the tapestry then, affirms suffering and cruelty as real. Violence and death are part of life. I know that I am alive because of my capacity to feel pain and know that I must die. 'I suffer, therefore I am.'[9]

ONLY THE SUFFERING GOD CAN HELP

But I look on the tapestry and see more than the suffering and death of one man, even everyman. It is this 'more than' which this suffering God. Quite simply, it demands my entire 'yes' to him:

> Love so amazing, so divine
> Demands my life, my soul, my all.

It demands – but it does not coerce or manipulate. My 'yes', to be worth anything, has to be free, welling up from inside me. The broken figure on the cross, in his powerlessness, can compel me to do nothing. Yet I find I am so involved in him that, more and more, I want to surrender everything. I sense the truth of the words John's Jesus utters as he approaches his cross: 'I, when I am lifted up from the earth, will draw all people to myself.'[14] I am drawn to him. I cannot escape him. My life, from now on, is bound up with the cross, or it is no life at all.

CRUCIFIED TRUTH

With great insight, Dostoevsky puts all this into the mouth of the Grand Inquisitor as he addresses Christ:

> You did not come down from the cross when they shouted to you, mocking and deriding you: 'If thou be the Son of God, come down from the cross.' You did not come down because . . . you did not want to enslave man by a miracle and because you hungered for faith based on free will and not on miracles. You hungered for freely given love and not for the servile raptures of the slave before the might that has terrified him once and for all.[15]

There are, I know from experience, two kinds of truth. There is the truth that compels allegiance and coerces. You cannot argue with the propositions of mathematics or logic. You could not argue (and this is the Grand Inquisitor's point) with stones turned to bread, or a Christ who came down from the cross. These would be certainties, leaving no choice but to accept them. There would be no freedom in the face of such black-and-whiteness, no room for faith. A lot of religion is increasingly like that. This bleak place is the subject of a Graham Greene nightmare:

> He had dreamed that Christ had been saved from the Cross by the legion of angels . . . So there was no final agony, no heavy stone which had to be rolled away, no discovery of an empty tomb. Father Quixote stood there watching on Golgotha as Christ stepped down from the Cross triumphant and acclaimed. The Roman soldiers, even the Centurion, knelt in His honour, and the people of Jerusalem poured up the hill to worship Him. The disciples clustered happily around. His Mother smiled through her tears of joy. There was no ambiguity, no room for doubt and no room for faith at all. The whole world knew with certainty that He was the Son of God . . . It was only a dream, of course . . . but none the less Father Quixote felt on waking the chill of despair felt by a man who realizes suddenly that he has taken up a profession which is of no use to anyone, who must continue to live in a kind of Saharan desert without doubt or faith, where everyone is convinced that the same belief is true. He had found himself whispering, 'God save me from such a belief!'[16]

The tapestry is, for me, the protest against coercive truth in all its forms. I feel in myself something of Father Quixote's chill of despair when someone tells me that God's existence is 'proved' by a healing miracle here or an answer to prayer there; or of an infallible Bible or an infallible church that leaves no room for any response but mute submissiveness in the face of a Deity who holds a theological gun at my head. You can perhaps fill pews that way, but you can never make *disciples*.

On the contrary, the tapestry's crucifixion is for me an image of this 'crucified truth' that draws me to make it mine. There is a silence in it that reminds me of the silence of Jesus to Pontius

Pilate's question, 'What is truth?'[17] Truth, it seems to say, does not demonstrate itself in words or actions that coerce. It discloses itself in vulnerability, in self-giving, in love. That is how the truth makes us free, the truth I see in Jesus: by inviting my faith in this lived reality, a reality I myself can begin to embody in the way I too understand and live my life. I am brought into a relationship with the Crucified.

AN OLD-FASHIONED WEAPON

So the violence beneath turns out to be a promise of peace. The death promises a new life, the shadow, a light about to dawn.

As I look again at the ashen, shadowy world at the foot of the tapestry, at the lonesome figure, and the funeral bier and pall below, another thought occurs to me. That too bespeaks the glimmer of dawn. The tension in the figure, the wooden cross-piece that seems to be pulled down by the very weight of God into an arc so incredible that I can scarcely believe the wood does not break under the strain – it is as if the cross, with Christ upon it, has become a kind of bow and arrow. There is a pent-up energy about it, a tautness, as if the crucified Jesus below is about to be catapulted through the figure of the man above into the glorified Christ who fills the tapestry. The poet says:

> The cross
> is an old-fashioned weapon, but its bow
> is drawn unerringly
> against the heart.[18]

Can I perhaps see a hint here that this human wreck on the cross is to become the one who faith says has overcome death and is alive for ever? Sometimes, when I see the crucifixions human beings inflict on one another, that 'perhaps' is all I am capable of, Thomas Hardy's 'hoping it might be so'. There seem to be many 'perhapses' when religion comes face to face with pain.

But at other times, I find I can rise above 'perhaps' to something more akin to Thomas the doubter's 'My Lord and my God!'[19] The Russian poetess Irina Ratushinskya, having endured the horrors of labour camp for many years, wrote a moving and radiant account of her experiences. Surrounded as she was by mockery, hatred and fear on every side, she and her friends were enabled to keep the fragile flame of faith alive. Her book is often in my mind as I contemplate this crucifixion on the tapestry, and my eye is then drawn back up, as it always is, to Christ in Glory above. She gave her book the title *Grey is the Colour of Hope.*

10

HEAVENLY BESTIARY:
THE FOUR LIVING CREATURES

I HAVE ALREADY written about the power of story as 'life-speaking'. My illustration came from the *Arabian Nights*. To me, it seems natural to turn to fairy tales and fantasy to illuminate and enrich life. I must have begun a lifetime's reading with this kind of literature. I still have (and read) the bulky black volume of *Grimm's Fairy Stories* that provided me with endless hours of delight as a child. It was not long before I came across the Greek myths and the Arthurian legends. In adolescence, I devoured science fiction. In my early twenties, I discovered Wagner, and was electrified by Furtwängler's great performance of the *Ring* cycle on record, which my theological tutor and I listened to over many afternoons. At the same time, I began to read the Bible in a new way and encountered in its pages the same mythic, mind-stretching power that had so captivated me as a child.

Symbol, story, imagination: I think I must have glimpsed very early on the importance of these for myself. I now understand a little better their significance for us all. Bruno Bettelheim[1], for example, applies a psychologist's insights to fairy tales and argues that they have a vital function in helping children grow up and face the dilemmas of adult living. He suggests that to deny children a rich fantasy life is to handicap them psychologically and spiritually. It would be like denying a person his or her dreams. From here, it seems to me, it is just a short step to the world of religion with its great universal images, and to the liturgy where symbol, story and imagination coalesce into the drama of our lives. 'To live symbolically,' said Thomas Mann, 'is true freedom.'

The tapestry is full of symbol, story and imagination. In its whole and in its parts, it draws on the rich veins of symbolism that have informed the paths of men and women for many

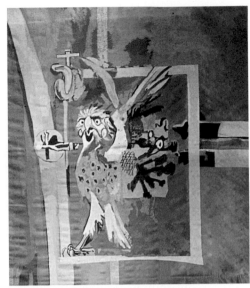

centuries. The tapestry is a Christian icon. It embodies much of the Christian iconography you find in classical Byzantine art;[2] yet many of its motifs are far older than the Christian faith, and indeed have meanings of their own which are familiar to people of very different religious traditions or even of no conscious faith at all. The light, for instance, at the top of the tapestry, or the chalice and serpent beneath the figure of Christ, or the struggle between good and evil symbolised in the conflict between Michael the Archangel and Satan – these are all universal human symbols before they are Christian ones. Perhaps, with Jung, I should call them archetypes, for they reside in the depths of our common human psyche, what he calls the collective unconscious. And it is of just these types of symbol that myth and fairy tale are made.

STORY-LAND CREATURES

The four living creatures around the throne of Christ belong, it seems to me, to this world of symbol, story and imagination. More than anything else in the tapestry, they are fantasy figures: creatures with wings, like Pegasus, or the gryphon, or the phoenix of legend. It is as if they have stepped out of story-land to give the tapestry a playful, imaginative aspect and to stop us taking it too literally. As I look at these beings, it is as if they are in constant motion, the four of them dancing around the centre of the picture in a fantastic ballet. Here is where the movement of the tapestry is, in marvellous counterpoint to the stillness of Christ at its heart.

But what does it mean, this square-dance of the four mythic creatures?

Like all symbols, the four creatures elude explanation. A symbol is not a sign, like a red traffic light, that means one thing and one thing only. A symbol opens up possibilities, draws me into its world, stretches my imagination, asks questions. I respond to a symbol at many different levels. Its perspectives are constantly shifting, even as I look at it. I can never say I have grasped its full meaning. That is its glory.

As I consider the four creatures, their significance seems to shift with their dance. They belong now to the Old Testament, now to the New; they echo the art of ancient Egypt, and are found on the great west portal of Chartres Cathedral; they are connected, it seems, with the four elements, the signs of the Zodiac, the four temperaments, the four winds, the four rivers of Eden; now they are about Christ, now about the created world, now about human life. They are indeed abundant carriers of symbol, story and imagination. Imaginative is the word I return to. Sutherland tells us that, in designing these creatures, he consciously moved away from 'realistic' depictions and the temptation to use well-worn 'heraldic' styles,³ to a final result that, to him, brought out each one's imaginative element.

I know, of course, that the four creatures around Christ are the traditional symbols of the four evangelists: Luke (the calf or bull), Matthew (the man), John (the eagle), Mark (the lion). That is to take them in clockwise order around the centre, as Sutherland intended. But I am not sure that is where I start from as I ponder them. What would they suggest to me if, for a moment, I were to lay aside the details of biblical imagery or the history of Christian iconography?

The artist helps me prime the pump of the imagination. He says,

> I tried to give each figure as much as I could its natural character: the predatory quality of the eagle, the ferociousness of the lion, the calm, bovine quality of the calf, slightly hysterical, very easily afraid and, in addition, the eagerness of the man . . . eager to understand, eager to feel, eager to see.⁴

At one level then, they are larger-than-life depictions of what they really are: creaturely, the handiwork of God in all its marvellous variety. 'Only through the demonstrations of their nature do animals pay unconscious tribute to the power which created them,' says Sutherland again. So the creatures belong with the tapestry's greatness. They represent and embody the aeons of the evolutionary process that brought life, movement and consciousness to birth. They belong to the world of green things we explored in Chapter 6. Their dance around the Creator is their homage to him. It epitomises the dance of the cosmos, the hymn of the universe, as it celebrates the glory of God.

I take my place in that square dance. I belong there, in the man, with the calf, the lion and the eagle, for we share this dignity of creaturehood. At least, we humans are intended to. The tapestry depicts creation in its rightness. The calf is truly a calf, the lion a lion, the eagle an eagle. Those great red wings speak to me of this quality of being as it should be, redeemed by the Christ who is the focus of the animals. The wings tell me they are truly alive with the life of God, free, themselves. So is the man truly himself, winged, alive, free to be God's. The tragedy of my life is precisely that I do not even aspire, much of the time, to this dignity of creaturehood. The animals achieve it spontaneously, naturally. By contrast I become, as we say, bestial (though I hesitate to use a word that seems to me to dishonour the animal world). I fall short of what I should be. My wings are clipped. I deny my own nature.

In Alnwick Parish Church, where I was incumbent, there is a series of four corbels in the south aisle that depict the progress of sin in a human life. The sin is gluttony. The first shows the sculpted face of an overfed man. In the second, his eyes have turned porcine; in the third, his nose has become a snout. In the fourth, he has turned into a pig. It is a powerful medieval sermon in stone, on the familiar text from the Old Testament that you become like the god you worship. 'To flatter the gods, it is enough to imitate them,' said Seneca. My dilemma is that I am pulled in both directions. I aspire to grow wings and fly. Yet I am at the same time dragged down into the mud. 'Wretched man that I am!'⁵ cries St Paul out of this experience that tears you in two. Who shall deliver me?

BEING BESTIAL, BEING HUMAN

As I continue to meditate on my state, caught between angels and dirt, between heaven and hell, it occurs to me to think of the four creatures as embodying aspects of myself. I come back to Sutherland's epithets: a fearful calf, an eager man, a predatory eagle, a ferocious lion. The tapestry makes me look at that 'animal' part of myself, those basic energies that drive me and make me, so largely, what I am. It is important that I face this difficult question. The journalist Janet Malcolm wrote a book in which she attempted, as a lay person, to get inside the world of psychoanalysis by talking to a group of North American analysts and their patients. One of her interviews led to a discussion about this 'animal' side of human nature. She quotes the analyst: 'To say that man is not an animal is to say nothing that banal people haven't always said. To say that our essential humanity resides in precisely that part of our nature which is most instinctual, primitive and infantile – animal – is to say something radical.'[6]

That is what the tapestry proposes I do: face reality in a radical way. The question is, are these 'animal' qualities in myself redeemed, or not? Unredeemed, untamed, the four creatures symbolise deep disorder and destructiveness, it seems to me. The calf, cowering, turning away from danger, 'slightly hysterical' is my cowardice, my lack of spirit, my tendency to run away from life's demands and hide, infantlike, in some imagined safe, dark place. The man, rushing headlong as if towards some abyss, is my overconfidence in my own ability, the assumption that I can rule the world through my reason, my technology or my strength. The eagle, looking for prey, is my oppressive side, ready to exploit those who are weaker than I am, impatient with weakness, vulnerability and compassion. The lion, in its ferocity, is my rage, my wildness, my untamed passion, my instinct for violence, my urge to dominate and hurt.

Seen in this way, it is a demonic bestiary. But – world, events continue to remind me – it is a truthful mirror of human life. If for the moment I took Christ out of the picture, and removed the creatures' wings I might detect in this circle of beasts, a reflection of Dante's hell where all our unredeemed, bestial qualities are seen for what they really are. It is the place where the masks are off and true faces are revealed. Those who have experienced the inhumanity of other human beings will tell us

life – they are interwoven. I look at them again, the four of them, drawn as if by gravity to Christ at the heart. 'Four' seems to symbolise completeness, wholeness; there is a mandala in the tapestry, with a still centre where everything is right and opposing forces are resolved. It is like the end of a fairy-tale. That meditation holds me and reassures me that this intermeshed story, God's and mine, is going to reach a climax. 'I am with you always, to the end of the age.'[9] The gospel preached to me by the four creatures tells me that I am on course, that the world is on course; that despite appearances, that point of divine closure when all is right between heaven and earth, when Christ is all – that 'omega point', as Teilhard de Chardin calls it, will come. 'All shall be well, and all shall be well, and all manner of thing shall be well.'[10]

DRAWN IN AND FLUNG OUT

But then another, contrasting metaphor occurs to me. In that still centre I see an infinite, pent-up energy, the cosmic forces that created the universe. And then it is as if the four creatures are flung out from it like constellations hurled into space by the Big Bang. I think of the gospels again and that vibrant message of the good news flung into the world by the 'big bang' of Easter. I see myself in that as well, two thousand years later, my story bound up with this Easter story, still being hurled outwards into human space to bring good news and healing. That is what we call mission. So the four winged creatures, icons of my own redemption, become icons of the world's too. They say to me that contemplation is only half of the spiritual life. There must be action, an outward thrust, involvement with the world, service of others, ties to the poor. Easter must come true in life. Christ must reign in glory in his world.

So the four creatures, it seems, are both drawn in and flung out. I am pulled to the centre by an attraction I cannot resist; yet at the same time flung out by the creative, resurrecting energy that is the source of this redeeming love. There is a paradox here, a tension. But it is the basic tension of Christian spirituality, of Christian living: a movement inward with its vision, its renewal, its recreating; and a movement outward to make that vision live in human experience. I find myself caught between these two fundamental movements all the time: into Christ, into the world. Perhaps it is as simple as saying that I bring to Christ my unredeemed, bestial qualities; and then, given wings, those same qualities that make me what I am are released, commissioned to serve the world and bring to it the healing, renewing power of that same risen Christ.

I am powerfully reminded of this every time I worship in the Cathedral. The great figure of Christ on the tapestry draws my mind and heart constantly as I look towards the altar, and the mystery of love being acted out there. But then, having received that mystery into myself as bread and wine, I turn round. I see ahead of me, not a blank west wall but a glass screen; and through it, the ruins of the old Cathedral and beyond, the city. I hear the words of dismissal: 'Go in peace to love and serve the Lord.' So I pass through the screen, crossing that threshold that is no threshold, so transparent is it, between worship and mission, between contemplation and action. I pass into the broken ruins of human life: the suffering, the pain, the conflict. I pass into the city: the place of work, endeavour and achievement. I bring with me the vision of Christ, Christ in me; and through me – for so I hope and pray – he becomes the man for others. The bread of eucharist becomes bread for the world. God's story, my story, the world's story become one. The Word is made flesh.

That is to anticipate the end of my meditation, when the time comes to turn away from the tapestry. But it is an important anticipation. This Lent, I pondered the enigmatic words with which St Mark describes Jesus' desert ordeal. He says only this: 'He was in the wilderness forty days, tempted by Satan; and he was with the wild beasts, and the angels waited on him.'[11] With Satan, with wild beasts, with angels, just as they are on the tapestry. Life in its totality seems there, and Jesus is 'driven out by the Spirit', Mark says, to immerse himself in it. What he does *symbolically* in the desert he proceeds to do *actually* in his ministry.

I find in that an image of Christian mission and involvement. Symbol, story and imagination – the tapestry, the liturgy or, in St Mark, the desert – merge into reality, for that is what they are *about*. I glimpse in worship and living, in prayer and in politics, a transforming presence. What is bestial is being made human, what is of demons, angelic. I begin to believe that it is not only fairy tales that have a happy ending.

11

WHO IS LIKE GOD?
ST MICHAEL AND SATAN

CALLED BY NAME

MY NAME is one of my treasured possessions. Over the years it has become part of me. I could not think of 'myself' as other than Michael. It is, I know, only a word; the sound of its two ordinary syllables belongs to millions of others beside myself, for it is one of the commonest of names. And yet no-one else hears it as I do. To me, it is part of my identity. It carries a unique set of memories and associations. I hear my parents calling me by name from before the dawn of consciousness; my grandmother, lovingly pronouncing it in her characteristic German-Jewish way; schoolteachers, doctors, neighbours, friends, most of whom I see no longer . . . my name brings so many echoes of them to mind. I hear myself called to, educated, cared for, told off, looked up to, looked down on, judged, affirmed, loved. I hear myself known, made vulnerable because others have got hold of part of me for good or ill.

This seems to me what the story in the Book of Exodus is about, when God discloses his name Yahweh to Moses. Moses removes his sandals, for the revealing of an intimate name is holy ground.[1] It is as if God is allowing his people access to his inner self by this disclosure of his name. It is the beginning of a deeply personal, intimate relationship. It is out of that covenant love that God says to me, 'I have called you by your name; you are mine.'[2] I have felt that when hearing myself addressed at some of those great moments in the life cycle: baptism, marriage, ordination. It is at those points of naming in the rites of passage that I felt myself both known and loved.

A PICTURE OF FAITH

over the border into Northumberland. It made sense, in a dangerous age, to invoke Michael, 'prince of the armies of Israel'.[4]

Coventry Cathedral is dedicated to him too. (True, the elevation on which it stands is not great, though there is an ancient alleyway running up to the old Cathedral called 'Hilltop' to prove that that is what it is.) The first thing you see as you come up the steps to the new Cathedral is the sculpture of St Michael and the Devil by Jacob Epstein in the last flowering of his genius. He features too (Michael, that is) on the great west screen by John Hutton, surrounded by other angels, and the saints of biblical and post-biblical times.

On the tapestry he appears, as it were, out of the side of Christ. He grasps hold of his adversary (which is what the word 'Satan' means), physically bundling him out, legs flailing, from the place where he no longer has a home. The battle, the Apocalypse's war in heaven, is already over. The field has been cleared of the carnage. Satan is defeated. He is cast out into the void, a pathetic, diminutive creature all but swallowed up by the vast, empty space.

There is violence here. It is not the only place on the tapestry where I see violence: its potential is there in the naked strength of the lion; its results are there in the wreckage of the crucified man. The violence of Michael the Archangel is more disconcerting to me, however, perhaps because it is actually portrayed as an event on the tapestry and, what is more, portrayed as taking place so close to the figure of Christ himself. A whole set of contrasts is set up in my mind: between stillness and violence, between mercy and wrath, between affirmation and rejection, between compassion and condemnation. The Christ says to me 'come' while Michael says 'go'; Michael's hands close a door which Christ's keep open. I am bewildered by these mixed messages. I believe that if I stay with these paradoxes and contemplate them, rather than try to reason them out, I will find a resolution. But for the moment, what I see puzzles me. Who is this archangel, whose name I bear, whose behaviour is so disturbing?

122

CAST DOWN TO HELL

Wilfred Owen, in one of his poems that, like so much of his poetry, goes unerringly to the heart of this issue of violence, opens up this theological gap still wider:

> I dreamed kind Jesus fouled the big-gun gears;
> And caused a permanent stoppage in all bolts;
> And buckled with a smile Mausers and Colts;
> And rusted every Bayonet with his tears.
>
> And there were no more bombs of ours or theirs,
> Not even an old flint-lock, nor even a pikel.
> But God was vexed, and gave all power to Michael;
> And when I woke, he'd seen to our repairs.[5]

This poem makes me wonder about how we use the Michael mythology in worship and preaching, in the way we understand the work of grace. The poet's archangel is a cruel, militant symbol of might without mercy, of naked power untempered by kindness. And much as I am exhilarated by the apocalyptic imagery of victory trumpets, the beating of a thousand wings, the battle cries and all the panoply of triumph, I am sure it is heady, even dangerous stuff. These intoxicating myths, unbalanced by other gentler ones, can wreak havoc when they begin to be acted out by an individual or a group.

Then the slogan 'in this sign conquer' becomes a call to arms, a holy war, a crusade. There are, I understand, extreme so-called Christian fundamentalists who would be prepared to blow up the Dome of the Rock in Jerusalem, a sacred site of Islam, in order to rebuild the Jewish temple on the foundations of Solomon's and so fulfil the biblical conditions which they say will usher in the second coming of Christ. There are those in the USA who apparently could contemplate a nuclear holocaust because it would herald the new heaven and the new earth. I have not met such people myself. But I well remember, as a student, preaching a sermon to a congregation of kindly but decidedly narrow Christians of a pronounced evangelical persuasion. I think my text must have been the parable of the sheep and the goats. Mercifully, some inner censor of the memory has made me forget what I said that evening. But an elderly lady, her face shining, came up to me afterwards and congratulated me for preaching so forthrightly about hell and the fate of the wicked. 'We need to hear much more of this sort of thing,' she said, 'how God demonstrates his victory by sending sinners to the place where they belong.'

I need to be honest here. These are real projections that the myth of St Michael carries. Part – I like to think most – of me wants to see good triumph over evil, love over hatred. But at the same time, another part of me hankers after triumphalism, needs to win and wants to punish. It alarms me how easily these unredeemed instincts come to the surface. The clamour right now, in the face of the relentless rise in teenage crime, is for harsher sentencing policies, which can be a thinly disguised code for uncritical vengeance. When I am in this mode, the myth of Michael plays right into my insecurity. I invest other people with the unacknowledged, projected, dark side within myself, put them into the role of Satan and proceed to cast them down to hell. The catalogue of those who have suffered in this way in our century is a bleak reminder of this tendency: blacks in South Africa; Kurds in Iraq; Jews in Hitler's Germany; Indians in North America; women, homosexuals, political dissidents the world over.

How can this propensity for hatred be redeemed? Or to put it more provocatively, how can I redeem the Michael myth and use it, not to reinforce my pathologies and prejudices, but to help me work creatively towards a healed, reconciled order of things?

'FATHER, FORGIVE'

A few years ago I visited the beautiful city of Lübeck in northern Germany. From many miles away, as you approach it, you can see its seven spires standing serenely above the fields of Schleswig-Holstein. Those spires have been a landmark for centuries. What took me there was an invitation to speak at the service of dedication of the last of Lübeck's churches to be rebuilt after the devastation of allied bombing in 1942. As I saw those spires, I tried to imagine what the people of Lübeck must have felt as they saw the heart of their great Hanseatic port burned out of her. In one of the churches, the sublime Marienkirche, I saw something that moved me profoundly. This great church had been rebuilt after the war exactly as before – with one exception. During the bombing, as the church burned, the bells in the southwest tower had crashed to the ground. I found that these bells had been left exactly as they had fallen nearly fifty years before: smashed, splintered, silent for ever. Around them, wreaths had been laid. And nearby was a Cross of Nails from Coventry, symbol of friendship and reconciliation.

I went back to those bells again and again to think. Here was Lübeck's equivalent to Coventry's bombed-out Cathedral ruins: a perpetual memorial, a place of recollection and reminder 'lest we forget', a silent plea for a better world order of peace and understanding. The wreaths and the cross seemed to say, as the sanctuary of Coventry's ruined Cathedral says, 'Father, forgive': not them, but us – me – for the part we – I – have played in making this world the unreconciled place it is. I still go back to those smashed, silent bells in my imagination, just as I sometimes sit quietly in the Coventry ruins to reflect, repent and pray. And as I come back to St Michael on the tapestry with this experience in mind, I find I learn to see the dragon-slayer in a new way.

This came home to me in a fresh way in 1990, the year when Coventry commemorated the 50th anniversary of the Luftwaffe air-raid 'Moonlight Sonata' that destroyed the city and Cathedral on the night of 14 November. At the service of remembrance and reconciliation, 1085 fallen oak leaves drifted down from the vault to lie around the high altar, one for every person killed in the raids. Meanwhile, the music of Beethoven's *Moonlight Sonata* filled the Cathedral as we all thought our own thoughts and remembered. But the poignancy of that moment was only given significance for me by what had already happened in the bombed-out ruins outside. Under a grey

November sky, one of the German airmen who had taken part in the raid had stood in front of the altar and laid a wreath there. I can only imagine what must have passed through that old man's mind as he thought back fifty years. I know that the words etched into the sanctuary wall all those years ago, 'Father, forgive', took on new significance just then. I pray that what I glimpsed that day will remain with me for life.

For in those words that have come to mean so much to me, 'Father, forgive', I learn to see the violence of St Michael in terms of the violence of the crucifixion. That 'violence beneath', it seems to me, interprets the violence above and puts it in a new light. St Michael is violent to evil; in the crucifixion, evil is violent to Jesus. And yet the cross is at the same time the most violent blow ever inflicted upon evil. By opening himself up to evil, becoming vulnerable to it, absorbing it, evil is robbed of its power. 'And death shall be no more; death thou shalt die' says John Donne in one of his greatest sonnets.[6] In St John's account of the passion, it is the twisted wreckage of the man on the cross that has the victory. Alone, he has taken on the darkness of the world and put it to death. His throne of triumph is the triumph of love. 'It is accomplished,'[7] he cries, as he overcomes the world and dies. Truly, *amor vincit omnia*: love conquers everything.

PASSION FOR LOVE

What the shattered bells of Lübeck and the ruins of Coventry tell me is that there is a force stronger than the violence human beings inflict on one another. In one sense, I know only too well that the victor at Lübeck, Coventry, Hiroshima, Auschwitz, Vietnam, Kuwait and Bosnia, is evil itself. We are all its victims; those names underline our failures. I pray, 'Father, forgive'. Yet in a deeper sense, I know that evil does not have the last word. 'As long as a soul remains in hell Christ remains on the cross,' said Origen. That moving and humble act of the German airman pointed to where true victory lay: not in oppression, inhumanity or war, but in mutual forgiveness, reconciliation and love. It is a long slow road, this road that love chooses to be victorious. There are many setbacks on the way, many disappointments. But love is patient. She has plenty of time. In her precarious way she will overcome the world. In the cross, she already has.

I look again at St Michael on the tapestry. I see him differently now. Gone is the image of crude, naked power. Perhaps it was never there. Perhaps I put it there. I can almost see Michael, not bundling Satan out of heaven, but holding on to him for all he is worth, trying to rescue him from his fate. He is like someone risking life and limb to stop a friend hurling himself off the edge of a precipice. It seems now that Michael is redeeming evil rather than banishing it, pursuing it with the violence of love, with his fierce compassion, with a mercy that burns. It is the same pursuit of love that I see on the cross; that I hear in the medieval stories of Christ's harrowing of hell. 'This thing of darkness I acknowledge mine,' says Prospero of Caliban in *The Tempest*. This mercy of Michael's reminds me of a beautiful rococo sculpture of the archangel by Mathias Gunther in one of the Berlin museums. It shows him bending down to Satan in the hour of defeat, paradoxically seeming both to fend evil off with his shield, but also wanting to listen to him with compassion, just as the Lord God came calling to the man and the woman in the garden, not to banish them from Eden but to be kind. I see that same compassionate quality in Epstein's sculpture by the west door of Coventry Cathedral. In that perfectly poised figure of the triumphant Michael, there is kindness in his face.

I see something else too. I said, at the beginning of this chapter, that Satan is almost swallowed up in the vastness of the void above which he is poised. I see now the spiritual, theological truth of this. Satan is one of the tiniest things in the tapestry. It is as if he is being diminished into nothingness, evaporating like an ice cube in a warm room. Dante's picture of Satan is of ice-cold, an absolute zero at the core of hell. For evil has no existence of itself; it is non-love, non-truth, non-being. Fill that void with the love of God and it exists no more. It evaporates.

In C. S. Lewis's fantasy *The Great Divorce*,[8] the redeemed wonder where hell is. They are shown that it is no more than a minute crack in the ground, a tiny ever-diminishing world that is unreal, utterly unsubstantial compared to the firm, trustworthy reality that is heaven. Heaven is. Hell is not. So I learn that the drama of life is not some combat between equally poised forces of good and evil. It is more like St Michael holding Satan so that his power to hurt is diminished. St Michael and the devil introduce the only asymmetry in the tapestry. It is as if evil distorts the picture, or tries to. Yet here, the distortion is minimal. Satan is simply too light, too evanescent, to make any final difference. In the redemption of evil, balance and symmetry are restored: distortion is dissolved away, melted you might say.

So the tapestry helps me to see the archangel as an expression of God's transforming love. In the Old Testament prophecy of Hosea, Yahweh is depicted as a bridegroom who has been wronged by his wayward bride. Far from banishing her to oblivion, this bridegroom, consumed by his own love, pursues her until he finds her, brings her home and restores her.[9] I see this passionate lover in St Michael, undefeated by evil, pursuing it to the corners of hell in order to heal, redeem and restore. Salvation is about bringing home: not simply in the hereafter, but now, as I learn to be more at home with God, more at home in his world and more at home with myself.

> Whether I flie with angels, fall with dust,
> Thy hands made both, and I am there:
> Thy power and love, my love and trust,
> Make one place ev'rywhere.[10]

The name 'Michael' – my name – asks a question. It means, 'Who is like God?' The tapestry speaks to me about a strength that works through weakness, a power that, in its vulnerability, is more powerful than all the forces of evil, destructiveness and death. It reveals a mercy that burns at the heart of things. It tells me love's nature and love's name.

12

CUP OF BLESSING:
THE CHALICE AND THE SERPENT

BY NOW it will be clear that, for me, the symbols of the tapestry convey many different meanings. Sometimes I see what the artist consciously intended me to see. At other times I see things quite differently, and perhaps in a less orthodox way. In the last chapter, I toyed with the idea of 'ambiguity' as an enriching way of looking at symbols and images: that, as we saw, is the word Graham Sutherland himself uses of his tapestry. The richness of a great work of art is that, like a jewel, it sparkles in so many directions.

Of all the tapestry's symbols, it is the chalice and the serpent beneath the feet of Christ that seem capable of meaning so many different things. Sutherland's book quotes the legend according to which, at the Last Supper, 'St John was handed a cup of poisoned wine out of which, at his blessing, the poison rose in the shape of a serpent.'[1] It goes on to point out that the chalice represents the blood of Christ, and refers to the St Michael passage in the Book of Revelation: 'And they overcame him (Satan) by the blood of the lamb.'[2]

If I start here, then the chalice and serpent depict the same thing as St Michael: the victory of God over evil. 'That it may please thee . . . finally to beat down Satan under our feet' prays the Prayer Book Litany, and that is what I see: evil beaten down under Christ's feet and ours. But the chalice makes it clear how this triumph is achieved. It is on the cross that evil is defeated, drained as Jesus drained the cup of his passion that was handed to him. On the tapestry, the chalice stands between St Michael and the crucifixion, and tells me that every victory over evil is the victory of love poured out. At every eucharist, this chalice seems to hover just above the high altar in token of this love that comes to search me out, find me and conquer.

THE GRACE OF THE CHALICE

I find this a deeply satisfying symbol. On the tapestry, it seems to offer a kind of still centre where so many forces converge. There is the movement of the lion and the ox on either side, the violence of the crucifixion below and the swirls of Christ's robe above. Yet the chalice seems to radiate not only light, but tranquility and peacefulness. And in itself, as a thing of beauty, the chalice reassures me, calms me down and puts me in touch with myself. I hesitate to theorise about this: I simply describe the satisfying experience of contemplating the chalice, of taking hold of the cup at the, eucharist, not only for what it contains, but for what it is in itself. 'The grace of the chalice', as the medieval theologians used to say, is a phrase that resonates with me.

I think there must be something profound at work here, some unconscious energy I am tapping into. I feel that what I am put in touch with is my instinctual, intuitive side; and that what is quietened down is my assertive, rational drive towards control, success and achievement. Traditionally, those two sides of the human psyche are called – not always very helpfully – masculine and feminine. What I am saying, as a man, is that I need to discover and celebrate the God-given, feminine aspect to my maleness, to recover the sense of being rooted and connected to all that lives and to the good earth that sustains me. The chalice is for me such a feminine symbol: a container like the sea from which I evolved, and like the womb which nurtured me. It is an integrating symbol, for it helps me to see the two sides of myself in proper relationship to each other. That is healing. It helps me to see too, how God is my Mother as well as my Father; the loving parent who, in Hosea's poignant maternal image, 'bends down' to put her breast to my lips and feed me.[3] I take the chalice at every, eucharist, and know that I am fed still.

THE GRAIL ON THE SUNBEAM

This chalice in mid-heaven used to capture my imagination as a young child. Among the myths and fairy-tales I loved so much, the Arthurian legend had a special place. I would read and re-read those wonderful stories in a version for children which, as I look back, distilled the magic of medieval romances in a unique way. I still have the well-thumbed volume with its woodcut illustrations; and as I read them to my own children I can recapture, a trifle nostalgically, that sense of thrill as I transported myself back to the days of the Round Table and its knights.

I loved all those stories, but my favourites were the grail legends. For some reason, those tales of knights captured by a vision and travelling to the ends of the earth in pursuit of it moved me much. Perhaps something in me was stirring already, some religious instinct, some inkling that life, for me, would mean my own grail-quest. Near the beginning of the story, the grail makes its dramatic appearance as King Arthur and his knights sit down at the feast. Here is how the great unknown 13th century chronicler tells it:

> When they were all seated and the noise was hushed, there came a clap of thunder so loud and terrible that they thought the palace must fall. Suddenly the hall was lit by a sunbeam which shed a radiance through the palace seven times brighter than had been before. In this moment they were all illumined as it might be by the grace of the Holy Ghost, and they began to look at one another, uncertain and perplexed. But not one of those present could utter a word, for all had been struck dumb, without respect of person. When they had sat a long while thus, unable to speak . . . the Holy Grail appeared, covered with a cloth of white samite; and yet no mortal hand was seen to bear it. It entered through the great door, and at once the palace was filled with fragrance as though all the spices of the earth had been spilled abroad. It circled the hall along the great tables and each place was furnished in its wake with the food its occupants desired. When all were served, the Holy Grail vanished, they knew not how nor whither.[4]

Often I would read no further, but relive that scene, daydreaming of the chalice gliding along the sunbeam, silencing human chatter, releasing magical scents, nourishing the knights with its mystic food. Later on, I discovered Malory, Tennyson, T. H. White's *Once and Future King*, and above all Wagner's music drama *Parsifal*. These all shed new light on the story. I learned to see the grail legend as a universal myth of human experience, a parable of life's quest. But that childhood enchantment with the grail has never left me. And as I look at the tapestry's chalice, caught at the intersection of gold bands of light, radiating its own sunburst, I seem to see the grail on its sunbeam, bringing blessing and joy. For me, it makes the eucharist glow.

THE GRAIL AS DESTINY

Let me explain how, as I contemplate the chalice on the tapestry, so many strands of my life come together.

First of all I see in it my destiny, the destiny of humanity. I come back to the metaphor of the journey. The grail legends are about journeys made in order to glimpse the profound reality the sacred vessel symbolises. These are difficult, painful journeys. The knights encounter obstacles that must be surmounted, hardships that must be endured. It is the familiar, fairy-tale motif of the ordeal the hero has to undergo in order to reach his prize. In the romances only three knights – Percival, Bors and Galahad – complete the quest, so demanding is it in terms not only of courage and endurance but of inward purity and truth as well.

I see in this my long march towards the vision of God, this hard, lonely journey I am committed to because I am a human being and a Christian. Those words of Kierkegaard come back to me both to haunt and to inspire: 'purity of heart is to will one thing',[5] in this case, to will to reach the destination and attain the destiny which St Paul calls 'the glorious liberty of the children of God.'[6] The grail-chalice symbolises both the journey and the destiny, for the grail is both the object of the journey and the nourishment that sustains me on it. Jesus is the Truth and the Life, but he is the Way as well. In the eucharist's bread and wine, I have a foretaste of that destiny, and I am given food and drink for the journey.

So the chalice represents my joyful destiny. But it stands for my painful destiny as well. In the grail legends, most of the knights met cruel suffering, many death, on the grail's account. The price of ecstasy, it seems, is pain. In the gospels, the cup that Jesus tells his disciples he must drink is the cup of suffering. The cup that he prays, in Gethsemane, may pass from him is the cup of death. The eucharistic cup of blessing is a life poured out, blood shed. 'God's Son,' says the collect, 'went not up to joy but first he suffered pain.'[7] In his painful destiny is my glorious destiny, his cup of suffering my cup of joy.

> Love is that liquor, sweet and most divine,
> Which my God feels as blood, but I as wine.[8]

Blood as love's elixir, heaven's ambrosia: it is the sweet paradox of Holy Week. But I know well enough that I too must drink his cup. The way to the grail is still the way of suffering. I can no more side-step this painful destiny than Jesus could. In the broken bread and poured-out wine, it is the mystery of my own suffering self that is upon the altar. The chalice presents me with the stark, bloody truth about discipleship:

> No wound? No scar?
> Yes, as the master shall the servant be,
> And pierced are the feet that follow me;
> But thine are whole. Can he have followed far
> Who has no wound, no scar?[9]

And if this chalice is not exactly poisoned (though it often feels so to me), the serpent in it at least reminds me that part of my fallen human destiny is to have my heel bruised as I travel the grail road.

TRANSFORMATION SCENE

But there is another insight here. For what is clear in the Arthurian romances is that the grail changes people. It touches them profoundly. In Wagner's version of the grail legend, it is Parsifal, the 'pure fool' transformed into the knight of the grail, who brings salvation: 'made wise through pity'.

The climax of the first act comes as the young, ignorant Parsifal enters the Castle of the Grail for the first time and witnesses the grail feast. When I first heard the famous 'transformation music' that marks the change of scene from forest to castle hall, I could not believe anything could be at once so powerful and mysterious. This music seemed to me to arise out of the very depths of myself, with its alternate swelling and dying away like bells, its magical shifts of harmony. I could see the young boy initiated into mysteries beyond telling, entering some holy of holies. 'I hardly move, yet so far I seem to have come,' he sings. And Gurnemanz, his holy guide, tells him: 'You see, my son, here time changes into space.'

The chalice symbolises a transformation scene that is both outward and inward. Outwardly, in the grail legends, there are two key transformations. There is the healing of the mortal wound which afflicts the guardian of the grail, the aged Fisher-King, and there is the removal of the curse that has lain upon the land during the Fisher-King's affliction, and has turned the fertile soil into a wilderness. So transformation affects a people, a society, a land. There is a solidarity in pain and suffering, and there is a solidarity in healing and redemption. 'As in Adam all die, so in Christ shall all be made alive,'[10] says the New Testament. Our destinies are connected, as we have already seen, whether for good or for ill.

So in the chalice on the tapestry, I see this social dimension of Christ's healing, the political and communal transformation that I long for. I see in it the new wine of the kingdom Jesus preached, the good news for the poor, release of captives, sight for the blind and freedom for the oppressed. I see the healing of humanity's mortal wound, the removal of the curse on the land. At every eucharist, I see in the chalice the world's hope, just as I see in the broken bread the world's pain. I learn to keep hope alive, to feed it, to hope against hope that out of these eucharistic loaves and fishes, so to speak, thousands may be fed, a world even. 'Bread for myself is a material question,' said Berdyaev; 'bread for my neighbour is a spiritual question.' The chalice, the Christian eucharist, the liturgy and prayer are fundamentally and urgently about justice, peace and human freedom.[11]

THE QUESTION

Inwardly, the grail legends speak of deep changes within all who come in contact with it. In many versions, the finder of the grail has to ask a question in order to set in train the redemptive sequence of events. Sometimes it is the question, 'Where is the grail?', sometimes 'Whom does the grail serve?' or even 'What is the grail?' The very meaning of the question may be obscure, let alone the answer. But only by asking it can transformation take place. It is the simplicity of Percival that enables him to ask it at all.

Yet through the asking of the grail question, there is not only redemption for king and land, there is a vision for the questioner too, a profound change, a healing within. It is as if the penny drops. The grail feeds each knight with the food he most desires; in other words, fulfils deepest human longings, meets heartfelt human needs. So I see in the tapestry's chalice a lovely symbol of the healing held out to me if I will only pause long enough to ask the grail questions, the life-questions: what is my life about? Who am I? Where am I going? Those questions put me in touch with lost parts of myself, for I look at the chalice and learn that I will never find wholeness, never glimpse salvation, until I have learned to look reflectively and critically at my own life.

This motif of asking questions by which life is lost or saved recurs in the stories told by ancients. In one of the most famous, Oedipus encounters the Sphinx on the road to Thebes. This monster guards the road and poses riddles to travellers passing by. Those who cannot answer her questions are devoured. Oedipus' question is to identify the creature that has four legs in the morning, two at midday, and three in the evening. The answer, of course, is a human being – in infancy, in maturity, and in old age. This response, runs the story, saves Oedipus from death and, more than that, delivers the land from the Sphinx's curse.

What fascinates me in this story is that it concerns human identity. The riddle of the Sphinx turns out to be a life-question, a grail-question: it is about who I am, this being on a journey from crawling babyhood through upright adulthood to stick-supported senility. It puts to me the all-important issue of my self-understanding, my awareness as a human being. If I can answer this elusive question, the story says, I am safe to continue my journey. If I fail the test, I am lost. It comes back to Delphi again, to knowing myself. 'The unexamined life is not worth living,' said Socrates.

I know this deep down, or believe I do. Yet I collude with pressure of work, demands of other people, the temptation to waste time in order to avoid the very thing that will lead to transformation, healing and growth. I need to give time to this life task if, to go back to the metaphor I used near the beginning of this book, I am to be an artist of my own life. The grail, the chalice, is a symbol of integration, of saying 'yes' to life and finding that, as Irenaeus put it, 'the glory of God is a human being fully alive.' The quest for the holy grail is the quest for God. But it is also the quest for myself. The two are not different. As I thirst for God, I thirst for my own self. As I find myself, I find God. As I drink from this chalice of new birth, of enlightenment, I know that I am discovering what my true end and purpose is. The Sphinx-question, the grail-question, begins to be answered. In the deep places of my being something stirs, and I know I am alive.

THE HEALING CHALICE

And there is a change in the serpent too. For I see him in a new way, no longer the poisoner of the chalice, the source of the curse. He becomes Aesculapius, the Roman god of healing whose symbol was the serpent because of its ability to shed its skin and regenerate itself. Or he becomes the bronze serpent, lifted up in the desert during the wanderings of the Hebrews, so that whoever so much as looked at it was healed. He becomes Christ himself who, St John's Gospel tells me, was 'lifted up' like that serpent, so that through him I might live.[12] The chalice and the serpent hold out that promise of eternal, abundant life, that new way of being fully alive that is the gift of God. They are a sign that there is joy as well as woe, that our human hurts can he healed and our deep yearnings fulfilled. They say to me that life is pure gift. They invite me to say 'yes' to God.

As this marvellous symbol hovers over our eucharistic celebration, I feel two things keenly. First, I feel the poverty of so much of the church's life and my own life. I am made aware of my falling short of God's glory; of my want of imagination, sweetness and warmth; of my lack of feeling and generosity. Often, perhaps usually, I am so dull of spirit that I have no real expectation that I might be moved and changed somehow, whether through the church's 'means of grace', or the holy-common sacraments of everyday life that are so freely given. I know my failure to earth my worship in life, and make connections between my spirituality and the political, social and human tasks that await me in the world. The chalice – the grail – speaks to me of all these things as I struggle with what the eucharist means: not only to me personally and 'privately', but to society, 'publicly'.

Early, on summer mornings, we celebrate the eucharist in the Chapel of Christ the Servant at the Cathedral. The Chapel is circular, a kind of glass cylinder with a very clear, pure light, transparent to the world outside. Once upon a time, you could look out from there across the city to the motor manufacturing plants that were Coventry's industrial life-blood. Now you look out, or rather *up*, at the University halls of residence and a big city-centre hotel. Sometimes, as we stand there making eucharist, I see curtains drawn back in students' bedrooms and wonder what our breaking of the bread is saying to those beyond the aumbry that encloses us. The Chapel is a very public place in which to 'proclaim', as Paul puts it in a strongly missionary turn of phrase, the Lord's death.[13] Is it the gospel that they see – 'public truth'? Or the esoteric private ceremonies of a sect doing little more than talking to itself? Those are questions that all churches need to ask of their liturgy as the century moves towards its turning.

But if the chalice puts its own grail-question to the poverty of so much with which I busy myself, it also speaks – more powerfully – of the richness and generosity of God in coming to meet and nourish me. There is nothing mean or churlish about the grace of the chalice. Like a mother, it gives without measure, not holding back, it drains itself to the very dregs as it pours its life into ours. I have long felt that the way we celebrate the sacraments needs to speak more eloquently about this mothering, feeding aspect. Tiny morsels of wafer-bread, a puddle in the bottom of the chalice – these are not adequate signs of generosity. Perhaps they symbolise all too clearly the limits we want to put around the unlimited grace of God.

There is a question in this generosity too, the most important grail-question of all. It is the question that determines whether we live and die. 'Simon, son of John, do you love me?' is the form in which it was put to a man who had fallen far.[14] For him, that question went to the roots of his being, unmasking everything a human being could hide behind. Yet with the question, this painful stripping of illusion, was proffered the gift: a new communion with God, a new destiny by which to glorify him. The only question that matters is this question the chalice puts to me: 'do you love me?'

My answer to it – and I want it to be a resounding 'yes!' – changes everything. And even if, sometimes, I can barely whisper that affirmation, I sense it is enough for God. He comes running to meet me as I stumble feebly towards him. The door is open, the table set. I have come home.

And as I receive that liquor which to God is blood but to me is wine, I sense rising up within me the only response I can possibly make: that of *eucharistia*, gratitude. This thankfulness is more than words, more even than something felt. It is something lived out of the core of my being, something to

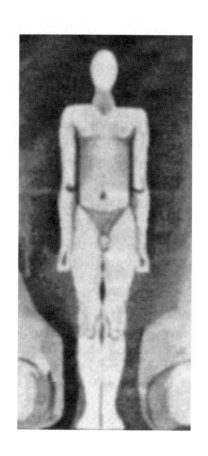

have felt most perplexed, crushed almost by the demands, dilemmas and uncertainties of being alive and human. At such times, it is as if I am stripped of all the normal securities with which I protect myself from too much reality. I am alone and naked in the dark, like the figure in the tapestry. Like Job, I hear a voice summoning me to stand up, like a man, and be questioned.[2] Those life-questions, the grail questions, demand to be heard: who am I? Why am I here? Where am I going? I must look the truth in the face. There can be no evasion.

I did not know, early on in my Christian experience, that this is a perfectly normal place to be, this place of darkness and unknowing – indeed, an important and even a good place, however painful. I can remember thinking, on offering my life to Christ and being baptised, that only light, laughter and glory lay ahead. My first experience of perplexity and loss of hope came as a shattering blow. I could not imagine it was possible, as a child of God, to feel the dark crushing me like this, to find myself yearning for what I had once had and seemed now to have lost. Well meaning but misguided friends put it down to the devil's temptations. They told me to read about the victorious Christian life and say my prayers more devoutly.

That was a long time ago, before I had got to know the Bible and learned of the universal experience of men and women of prayer down the centuries. I can remember that the story of the Transfiguration came as a revelation to me. In that story I learned the fundamental religious truth that the place of ecstasy and glory, where everything is transfigured and glows, is also the place of perplexity, confusion and fear. For the three disciples, the mountain-top experience of seeing the splendour of Jesus is suddenly overtaken by its opposite. 'A cloud came and overshadowed them,' says St Luke, 'and they were terrified.'[3] In an instant, the light is put out; their peak experience is no more than a remembered glow. Now, they grope around in terror as the cloud overwhelms them. They see Jesus no longer. He is hidden from them just as, later on in Luke's story, another cloud takes the risen Lord from his anxious disciples and – except to the eyes of faith – he is gone for good. I have already touched on this perplexing hiddenness of the God Luther called *Deus absconditus*. It is as much a fact of religious experience as his revealedness. What is more, if the biblical story and my own experience are any guide, it is precisely at times of my spiritual 'highs' that cloud and darkness are likely to sweep around me, and I am the man on the tapestry again, alone, a 'little boy lost', naked, wondering.

STRUGGLING IN THE NIGHT

The story that comes closest to epitomising this experience for me is the account in Genesis of Jacob's encounter at Penuel under the night sky. This story is so full of this feeling of perplexity, struggle and dark night, that I must quote it in full:

> The same night he arose and took his two wives, his two maids, and his eleven children, and crossed the ford of the Jabbok. He took them and sent them across the stream, and likewise everything that he had. And Jacob was left alone; and a man wrestled with him until the breaking of the day. When the man saw that he did not prevail against Jacob, he touched the hollow of his thigh; and Jacob's thigh was put out of joint as he wrestled with him. Then he said, 'Let me go, for the day is breaking.' But Jacob said, 'I will not let you go, unless you bless me.' And he said to him, 'What is your name?' And he said, 'Jacob.' Then he said, 'Your name shall no more be called Jacob, but Israel, for you have striven with God and with men, and have prevailed.' Then Jacob asked him, 'Tell me, I pray, your name.' But he said, 'Why is it that you ask my name?' And there he blessed him. So Jacob called the name of the place Penuel, saying, 'For I have seen God face to face, and yet my life is preserved.' The sun rose upon him as he passed Penuel, limping because of his thigh.[4]

This story has many archetypal aspects to it: the water, the night, the struggle, the nameless adversary, the renaming of

144

Jacob. As the book of Genesis unfolds, it is clear that this Penuel experience is a rite of passage for Jacob. It seems to mark a turning point in his understanding of God. From now on he is a new man, with a new name: 'Israel'; the brook Jabbock is the water of baptism out of which he emerges with his new name and new identity. As he does so, the sun rises; darkness flees; it is a new dawn, a new beginning, a new life. Israel has seen God.

What is so powerful here is the storyteller's boldness in overturning the expectations I as reader bring to this kind of tale. The story says that to see God at Penuel means night, not day; darkness, not light. It says that to encounter him means standing utterly alone and naked beneath the night sky. It says that when I confront this mysterious, dreadful, nameless Being, I will find not comfort but struggle, not ease but pain. I will find him to be a God who hurts before he heals, confuses before he enlightens, wounds before he blesses. And when the sun finally rises, I shall be maimed for life, limping away into the light. This is the violent mercy of Michael the archangel again. The story tells me that it is precisely in my struggles, my conflicts, my doubts and my darkness that I can expect to meet this God who hides himself. 'I have seen God face to face,' says Jacob of this nightmare, 'and yet my life is preserved.' The human being on the tapestry, standing alone in the darkness is for me the individual, the community, the nation that feels itself to be struggling under the night sky.[5]

In this figure, this Jacob-in-the-darkness, I have three things to learn. I learn for a start that I need not be afraid of my own nakedness, that is to say, my own human nature as it is exposed to be. The sad fact is that through laziness or fear I do not know nearly enough about my own naked self. It is said of the Greek philosopher Solon that he was asked by a stranger whether he knew a man called Solon. 'I know him, but not well,' Solon replied. I know myself – but not well. I know a little about my personality type, my strengths and weaknesses, my loneliness, my emptiness and my pain. But I know much less about 'the violence beneath': my repressed urges, my anger, my capacity for violence and my hate. All these lurk in some unexplored deep place in my psyche. They belong to the shadow; they are part of the night.

The spiritual tradition seems to me to be saying that a primary task of spirituality is self-knowledge. In my meditation on the tapestry, this is coming to be a constant theme. One of the great classics of English spiritual writing is the 14th century work of an anonymous writer, *The Cloud of Unknowing*, where I find this advice: 'Therefore swink and sweat in all that thou canst, for to get thee a true knowing and a feeling of thyself as thou art; and then I trow that, soon after that, thou shalt have a true knowing and feeling of God as he is.'[6] This task is not to 'know myself' as some kind of end. It is unearthing the 'whys' of existence that the grail-question is concerned with. The Grand Inquisitor is once again a guide to perplexed souls: 'The mystery of human life is not only in living, but in knowing *why* one lives. Without a clear idea of what to live for man will not consent to live at all.'[7]

Secondly, I learn not to be afraid of praying with the whole of me, that is praying with whatever is brought to the surface by my self-discovery. My task is not only to know myself, but to integrate that knowledge into the totality of my life. As I pray, so I am. In the New Testament, the sin Jesus constantly condemns is that of hypocrisy, literally 'play-acting' – for the 'hypocrite' is the actor who dons a mask to go on stage, and so covers up his or her real self, his or her nakedness. Jesus teaches me that the God he calls 'Abba, Father' (and invites me to do the same) 'sees in secret'.

So I must learn to harness even that unknown, threatening part of me in the activity of prayer. The Psalms are my inspiration here. In this incomparable collection of Israel's praises and laments I find prayer expressing the entire spectrum of human emotion. I find celebration, thanksgiving, adoration and love. I find trust, acceptance, resignation and assurance. But I also find prayer interwoven with degrees of anger, hatred, despair and vengefulness that I barely recognise within myself. So burning with intensity are some of the psalmists' outpourings that many liturgical editions of the psalter bracket them out or omit them altogether as unsuitable for use in worship. Yet to me, to find this deeply felt emotional life canonised within the psalter is to say something profoundly important. It indicates that previous generations were not as coy as we are in censoring or sanitising our more intense feelings: perhaps they felt more confident than we do that our entire humanity is acceptable to God. As I recite these psalms, I am reminded of the startling insight of the Trappist Rule, that the liturgy makes us say things to God that we would not dare to say for ourselves. 'What will God do with those who have never wept?' asked John Donne: what will he do with those who have never allowed themselves to feel in his presence, whether joy or woe?

Thirdly, I learn to find God in this darkness. For Jacob, the adversary who wounds turns out to be the friend who blesses. The darkness is alive with God – but in ways that, to Jacob, are at first enigmatic. This God behaves in unexpected ways, guards his own mystery and remains elusive. The important thing is that Jacob is thoroughly changed by this encounter. Gone are his old, simplistic ways of understanding God. His limp is a lifelong sacrament of an experience of what Rudolph Otto described as *Mysterium tremens et fascinans*,[8] that which baffles, transcends, overwhelms; yet for all that is to be encountered, worshipped and loved.

THE NEGATIVE WAY

I must pursue this discovery of God in the darkness. Jung once said that our intense negative emotional experiences such as rage, depression, breakdown, even insanity are, in an important sense, religious experiences because they put us in touch, uniquely painfully, with parts of ourselves from which we are usually protected. I know that it has been at times of pain, sadness or depression that I have felt with a particular clarity; I have been at my most creative at these times, finding myself writing poetry, for example, which otherwise comes only with great difficulty. Life's painful experiences are like the sorrowful mysteries of the rosary: they are a bitter but real means of grace.

Like Jacob, they take me across black waters under a night sky; there is a conflict and a wound. I emerge limping, battered, exhausted, yet changed. I see things in new ways. I learn that, in the words of the medieval writer, I can pierce the darkness above me, 'smite upon the thick cloud of unknowing with a sharp dart of longing love,'⁹ and know God afresh. In my lostness, I find. In my not-having, I am made rich.

What I am describing is known as the 'negative way' of spirituality. It is a demanding way because it invites me, in effect, to renounce my own capacity to think about or describe God and instead to discover him in the naked experiences of silence, darkness and solitude. For the poet, a pilgrimage to a remote place brings him face to face with his life-question, his grail-question:

> They are just
> here with only the one question
> to ask, which life answers
> by being in them. It is I
> who ask. Was the pilgrimage
> I made to come to my own
> self, to learn that in times
>
> like these and for one like me
> God will never be plain and
> out there, but dark rather and
> inexplicable.¹⁰

The lonely man on the tapestry embodies this for me, with that great weight of dark shadow pressing relentlessly down above his head. Yet this *via negativa* is also the way of paradox.

> To learn to love
> is to be stripped of all love
> until you are wholly without love
> because
> until you have gone
> naked and afraid

into this cold dark place
where all love is taken from you
you will not know
that you are wholly within love.[11]

That is the paradox: that it is as I surrender to this emptiness that I find it to be filled. I am 'wholly within love'; the darkness that seemed so hostile turns out to be, in Henry Vaughan's phrase, the 'deep and dazzling darkness' of God himself. The cloud that swallowed up Christ on the mountain of transfiguration still contains him and shines because of him. It becomes the *shekinah*, the cloud of glory. In the absence is a profound presence. And as I pierce through to that presence, I find out that its nature and its name is Love.

THE DARKNESS OF GOD

The tapestry beautifully expresses this paradox. For the man's darkness is none other than the shadow of the great Christ above him. The fearful cloud over his head is the very skirt of Christ. On each side are the feet of Christ, strong, trustworthy. The man may not know it, but he is 'wholly within love'. I see myself in him now in a new way: erect, noble, dignified in this new status as child of God. He is as I know myself to be: 'wholly within love', held firm, profoundly safe.

I said to my soul, be still, and let the dark
come upon you
Which shall be the darkness of God . . .
So the darkness shall be the light and the
stillness the dancing.[12]

In this dark yet good place I can be still; and discover that I am dancing in the sunshine.

Yeats was not to know, when he wrote 'The Second Coming' early this century, how its succeeding decades would bear out his depressing analysis. I can pinpoint my own youthful awakening to the fragility of things quite accurately. It was the Cuban missile crisis of 1962, and the assassination of John F. Kennedy in 1963, that marked the end of my childhood and drowned my innocence. I knew then that my inner chaotic experience of puberty mirrored an outer, more public chaos. I sensed, though not in Yeats' words, that the centre might not hold.

In 1968 there came a small but vivid symbol of this fragility I saw in the world around me. In that year, the culmination of the sixties era, I left school and, before going to university, spent spring and summer in southern France working in an orphanage. While I was there the country was thrown into chaos as a result of the student riots. Everything ground to a halt. One day in May or June I took a bicycle and cycled south down the Rhone valley towards the sea. Before long I crossed the main Paris-Marseille railway line. I was astonished to find it already rusted over, with weeds beginning to grow between the tracks. So soon, I thought, do the tracks of human civilisation and achievement begin to disintegrate. I felt gloomy about the future of humanity as I stared down in the hot sunshine at those forlorn, silent rails. We are walking on eggshells, I thought; entropy is everywhere at work, the slide from cosmos back into chaos, putting creation's clock back to the beginning. 'Things fall apart, the centre cannot hold.'

That is my fear as I leave the edges and move in towards the centre. I need to know that there is something there; and that I can trust it. I need to find that the centre holds.

THE TREE AT THE CENTRE OF THE WORLD

One Easter I spent many hours in the Cathedral nave keeping the Great Vigil through the night until dawn. That night of waiting is the holiest in the year for Christians. You enter the darkened church on the evening of Saturday, the tapers of worshippers forming little points of light in the huge expanse of dark, the Easter Candle leading the way to proclaim the light of Christ. But the full splendour of Easter is not yet. That comes with the rising of the sun and the joyful meeting with the risen Lord at the first eucharist of the Day of days. Until then, you wait in the darkness. The church is like a cave, like the tomb in which the body of Jesus was laid. I sensed that very powerfully that particular Easter. Sometimes I sat in the nave, sometimes I lay on the marble floor, sometimes I walked around. The only light, apart from the glow of street lamps outside, was the Easter Candle on its stand, burning steadily through the night.

In this half-light, the tapestry lost its glow. It was there, of course – even at night, its presence overwhelmed. But the centre, the mandorla around Christ, appeared in quite a new way to me. It was as if the great almond shape surrounding him was a coffin; as if on Easter Eve, the tapestry portrayed him as buried, yes, and myself with him between his feet. I had never thought of Christ *lying* in the tapestry before, only sitting or standing. And now, as I look at him, the perspective still shifts. Now I am looking up at him risen, glorious, triumphant; now I am looking down on him in his coffin, noble, dignified, yet with the marks of his mortality still red and raw on his feet and hands. And around his body I see in the deep violets and purples, as it were, the hues of death, the colour the sky goes when there is a total eclipse of the sun.

In one way, this is what I find as I move in towards the centre. At the core of creation, at the centre of human life, I find the hues of suffering and death, the eclipse of the sun, what the poet calls 'the heartbreak at the heart of things.'[3] Underneath the greens and golds and reds of life, I come to a coffin. Put that way, it sounds melodramatic. But it is only the same truth that I see in the crucifixion panel put in a striking way, that Christ is crucified at the heart of his own creation; it is there that he is dead and buried. The ancient map makers used to depict the world with Jerusalem and the hill of Golgotha at its very centre There is a deep theological truth in those maps.

Seen in that way, my question, my grail-question as to whether the centre can hold remains a question. Christ buried at the heart of the tapestry, the 'heartbreak at the heart of things' that is our universal human experience, seem to speak of a centre that cannot hold, of inevitable collapse back into chaos and a final turning out of the light. But if I come back to the crucifixion, that tree at the centre of the world, I am reminded of the old Norse myths that told of the world ash tree, Yggdrasil, that held the universe together and kept it alive. The New Testament tells me that the cross is such a tree, a world tree, its wood proclaiming life through death. Easter says that on the third day, tomb became womb: an empty tomb became the womb of creation out of which sprang new life, a new world. Things do not fall apart after all.

TOMB AND WOMB

A death that is also a birth, the tomb becoming womb, that is a powerful insight the mandorla of the tapestry suggests. It makes me think of some of the holiest times of my life. I think I first experienced what, at the time, felt like creation holding its breath when I helped bring our first child into the world. It was a long labour, an all-night job. It was like the Easter Vigil – a time of waiting in hope in the silence. Next morning, we had a daughter. As I held her for the first time I drew into myself, contentedly, the familiar hospital smells – scents of cleanness and care – and I thought, these are good smells. Even now, the smell of a hospital that induces fear in some people only recalls for me the goodness, the God-givenness, of that birth-day. It makes me thankful.

I described in an earlier chapter how several years, and three more children later, I sat at the bedside of a parishioner who was dying. She had lived long, had been loved by her family and friends; her dying was natural and right. Her devoted husband had asked that she come home to die; now, in her last hour as life slipped away, I joined him to say farewell. She was unconscious. All we could do was wait. Again, it was night time; again, it felt like the holy night of Easter. But the memories that came flooding back during those hours of waiting were the memories of my daughter's birth. Here, at the other end of life, was the same feeling of holiness, a passage, not so much from life to non-life but one kind of life to another. It felt like the place of a birth: a place to be thankful, to be hopeful; a place to gather up pasts and futures and offer them to God. Tomb and womb, I saw, belong together. 'It is in dying that we are born again to eternal life.'[4]

So the mandorla is a symbol of birth as well as death. Indeed, the almond was an ancient image of birth, because of its womb-like shape. Perhaps it recalled the sea shell, another primordial symbol of fertility and birth, as in the myth of the birth of Aphrodite, stepping from her scallop-shell onto the shores of Cyprus. Wherever she walked, it was said, flowers sprang up in her footsteps. The Sioux Indians have a lovely saying that where the Great Spirit has stopped and touched the earth, something grows. This womb at the centre of the tapestry, filled with its dark waters, as I see it in this light seems to be filling the rest of the huge icon with life, this burst of love at its heart somehow touching everything else, causing it to glow green or red or gold. It is like the great world-egg in primitive mythology which, when hatched, becomes the living universe. Perhaps there is an echo of this in Genesis where the Spirit of God 'hovers' (a feminine participle) over the face of the deep like a dove hovering over her young. Where Christ is born, all is life and love.

But I am not yet ready to let go of this double perspective in the mandorla, this almond shape that is both death and birth, tomb and womb. My experience tells me that life's passages are of the same order of holiness. I wait for a death, and it is as if I wait for a birth. But the opposite is true as well. In birth, there is a kind of death, too. Not long before he died, John Donne preached what many of his listeners took to be his own funeral sermon.

We have a winding sheet in our mother's womb, which grows with us from our conception, and we come into the world wound up in that winding sheet, for we come to seek a grave. We celebrate our own funeral with cries, even at our birth . . . We come into a world that lasts many ages, but we last not.[5]

My icon of the Incarnation, at home, has the infant Jesus wrapped in a winding sheet, the cave of his birth foreshadowing the cave of his tomb. His destiny is mine: like him, I am born to die, as the tapestry has already taught me in more ways than one. The tapestry is an icon of my whole existence. It is as if I emerge from the womb of the mandorla, flung out into life like the four living creatures, only to return finally into those indigo waters, taken back whence I came, earth to earth, ashes to ashes, dust to dust. In birth, in life, in death, I come from God, live in God, return to God – that is what the Christ at the centre of the dark mandorla edged with gold says to me. My life is hid with Christ in God.

DYING WE LIVE

In his poem 'The Journey of the Magi', T. S. Eliot imagines the Epiphany travellers from the east reflecting afterwards on what they had experienced at their 'cold coming'.

> Were we led all that way for
> Birth or Death? There was a Birth, certainly.
> We had evidence and no doubt. I had seen birth
> and death,
> But had thought they were different; this Birth was
> Hard and bitter agony for us, like Death, our death.
> We returned to our places, these Kingdoms,
> But no longer at ease there, in the old dispensation,
> With an alien people clutching their gods.
> I should be glad of another death.[6]

'I had seen birth and death, but had thought they were different.' This is the insight I have been struggling towards as I look at the mandorla, tomb and womb. I had once thought they were different. Experience, suffering and prayer tell me they are not. 'It was a long time ago, I remember,' says Eliot's speaker, and this 'long time ago' is important, for it clarifies things, helps to restore perspective. At this distance I learn to see birth and death, like Blake's joy and woe, as 'woven fine'. Events that seemed like a birth or rebirth contain the fibres of death while those that, at the time, appeared only to be a dying of some kind turn out to be shot through, or at least edged, with the promise of new life.

And that is supremely true of the process, the dynamic, of Christian living that is called discipleship. The journey of the magi, in Eliot's great poem, is a metaphor of Christian conversion. It tells the story of human beings drawn to the Christ, drawn to the centre, if you like. There is a long, hard journey towards discovery, towards the finding of what is new-born, the recent gift of the womb. And in the finding is another birth, a regeneration. I come to Christ, and find that he is born in me anew, the Word made flesh in the particular, historic, unique human being that is myself. I am no longer at home in the old dispensation, among the alien gods I once worshipped, whatever they ate. Conversion, *conversio*, means literally, 'turning round'. It is a powerful metaphor of changing direction in life, or being turned round, so inescapable is the Christ who demands our allegiance, as in the case of Saul of Tarsus on the Damascus Road. It is a kind of being born, the 'new birth' the Fourth Gospel calls it. Without it, says Jesus to Nicodemus, we cannot see the kingdom of God.[7]

But is it only a birth? There is a birth, certainly. We have evidence, and no doubt. At the time, those meetings with Christ in a new way feel like being born (or how I imagine it must feel). There is a freshness, a newness about everything, a surge of energy, the sap rising. 'Conversion' is not a once for all happening. I am all the time being 'turned' back to Christ, tied back to him (the meaning, as we saw earlier, of the word 'religion', or it should be if the Christian life means anything). And each new experience of him, each new conversion, feels like a birth. I begin to believe St Paul's words, that we are changed 'from one degree of glory to another'. The grail transformation is lifelong.

Yet there is a death too. 'It was a long time ago, I remember,' that I was baptised a Christian as a teenager. Then it felt like a birth. Now I see it as a death too, a renunciation of an old life, of old attitudes and old gods. The womb of the baptismal waters was also the tomb in which my old, unalive self was buried. 'Dead to sin, and alive to God through Jesus Christ our Lord'[8] is the New Testament's powerful account of baptism. The baptismal liturgy pictures it in the images of the great Old Testament stories of deliverance: the corrupt, antediluvian world drowned in the flood; the Hebrews leaving behind them their Egyptian slavery as they crossed the Red Sea for a life of freedom. And supremely, of course, it is the death and burial of Jesus into which I must enter in baptism if I am to rise victorious with him to share his Easter life.

EASTER DAWN

So I come back to the Easter Vigil, that night that is both dying to the old and rising to the new. In the tomb of the dark church, with hours of watching, waiting and reflecting, the slow march of the hours and minutes towards a dawn you think will never come, there is time to review your life, time to ponder what needs to be died to, time to look for the signs of new life. In the liturgy of Easter Eve, light and dark, life and death, joy and woe are 'woven fine'. And then, in the baptismal rite that is central to the Easter liturgy, there is offered the annual liturgical re-enactment of *conversio*, this turning to the risen Lord, this pledging of faith and trust and loyalty in him for another year. The tomb of the church becomes the womb of the Easter life; the waters of baptism, like the four rivers of Eden, flow to the four corners of the earth. You know, in a sense beyond reason or argument, that the tomb is empty of Christ; that this womb has given birth to the new creation, and death is swallowed up in victory.

And as the Easter dawn lights up the tapestry once more and its colours return, I see all this in the mandorla: the indigo waters of baptism that are both death and life; the tomb of Christ that is also the womb of Easter; the golden light around the edges that is the radiance of a never-setting sun. And I come to see that what is true of Easter Day is true of every day. Things come together in this gift of an Easter vision. There is a point of convergence, of focus. The centre holds!

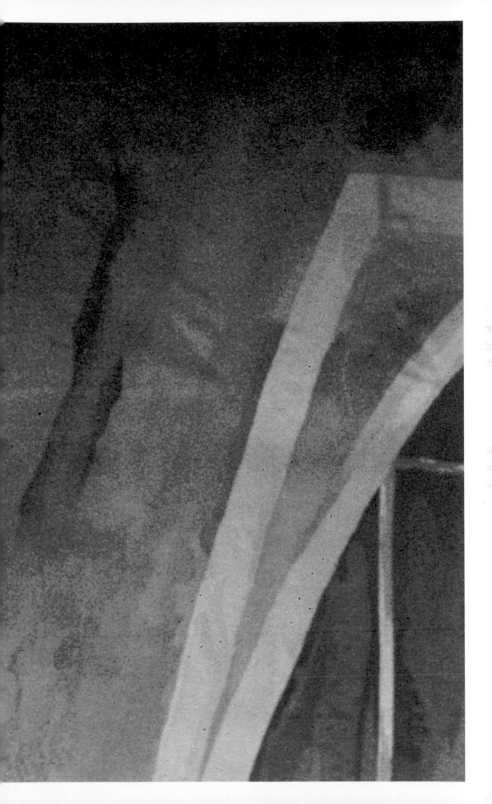

15

AT THE CENTRE:
'BEHOLD THE MAN'

I COME TO the heart of the tapestry to find out what is at this centre that holds – holds in itself, and holds the fabric of the universe together. And at once I have the impression of shadows fleeing away. It is as if everything else on the tapestry is a symbol of some other deeper reality, leading into 'the heart of things' in its own unique way. The truth of these symbols I have been exploring – the colours, the light, the chalice, the four living creatures and so on – is the oblique, analogical truth of the image, the metaphor.

> Tell all the truth, but tell it slant –
> Success in Circuit lies
> Too bright for our infirm Delight
> The Truth's superb surprise.

said Emily Dickinson in a marvellous epigram.[1] That is what most of the tapestry does. It beckons to me, entices me into its life by opening up this symbolic world of the imagination, cleansing the doors of my perception. But when I come to Christ in glory, images and symbols, things that stand for something else, vanish away. He can only stand for himself. There is no other reality. 'When the complete comes, the partial shall come to an end,' says Paul.[2] I see Christ, as it were, full-frontally, face to face, stand beneath his gaze and know that I am searched out to the very core of my being. I am known.

How each of us respond to that searching gaze says a great deal about ourselves. Here, more than anywhere else, what matters is not the intention of the artist. What matters is how I see Christ, and how I believe his gaze sees me. What matters are

those grail-questions that are asked in this meeting of Christ's eyes and mine, the questions about life and love and destiny. I know that this encounter will judge me before it saves; for in my being known there will be an exposure, possibly a cruel exposure, of the truth about myself. There is a 'wound of knowledge' that must hurt in order to heal:

The wounded surgeon plies the steel
That questions the distempered part;
Beneath the bleeding hands we feel
The sharp compassion of the healer's art
Resolving the enigma of the fever chart.[3]

This is a bitter mercy I must become open to. As Bonhoeffer says, there is no 'cheap grace', no easy, comfortable way to the healing knowledge of God and of myself. The marks of pain in the hands and feet of Christ on the tapestry show me that he is always a wounded healer and, I must learn, a wounding healer too, inflicting the necessary injuries that his 'sharp compassion' demands. The Book of Proverbs says, 'Faithful are the wounds of a friend'.[4]

RECOGNITION

The face of Christ is, for me, the most powerful part of the tapestry. As I have said, it seems to follow me round the Cathedral, holding me and demanding my attention. It is a miracle to me that out of inanimate warp and weft could be created such a presence, something so alive, so searching. I imagine that it must be the most difficult thing in the world to depict the face of Christ convincingly: to get the right harmonies of divinity, humanity, kindness, justice, majesty, humility and glory. I think I know this convincing quality when I see it in the Christs of Piero della Francesca, Rembrandt, El Greco, or in the frescoes of Florence or the sculptures of Chartres. I think I know it because of a quality I miss in so much popular religious so-called art: the quality of *recognition*. I don't only mean whatever has gone on inside the artist as part of the creative process, his or her own recognition of Christ. I mean that quality by which there is a crossing over, a meeting of eyes and spirits, a sense of being searched, questioned and known, in order that I too may search, question and know for myself.

Sometimes, as I come into the Cathedral for morning prayer, I feel this presence, this mutual recognition so strongly that I want to salute it and him; offer a greeting, say good morning. And if I feel slightly foolish, I remind myself that even in saying good morning to my friends and colleagues, I am also saluting Christ in glory in them. I wrote earlier about the icon on the wall, and icon in every human being. Greeting is an act of reverence and recognition. The little courtesies of friendship we show one another are also acts of courtesy to God.

Three great recognition scenes from the New Testament come to mind as I ponder the face of Christ on the tapestry. As so much of the tapestry speaks to me of Good Friday and Easter, it is perhaps not surprising that they come from the passion and resurrection accounts in the gospels.

First I seem to see that moment in the house of Caiaphas, when Peter denies Jesus the third time.

> At that moment, while he was still speaking, the cock crowed. The Lord turned and looked at Peter. Then Peter remembered the word of the Lord, how he had said to him, 'before the cock crows today, you will deny me three times.' And he went out and wept bitterly . . ."[5]

That little cameo is like one of those bird or animal miniatures by Thomas Bewick, etched with razor sharpness. I see in Christ's face that look that penetrates right through, that knows the confusion, the fear and the guilt within me and above all, the sense of failure, of having let him down. I see judgement there. I know I am small, and spoiled. Like the soul of the dead man in Newman's poem *The Dream of Gerontius*, I want to cry out, as I meet the gaze of Christ, 'Take me away!' and, like Peter, to go out in the darkness and weep. Yet something keeps me inside; for there is compassion in that face too, understanding.

I know that if I cry out 'Christe eleison', Christ have mercy, I shall be heard. In the recognition of who I truly am, 'thou art the man!'[6] the possibility of forgiveness and reinstatement is lovingly held out. I see not only Jesus turning to gaze on Peter in the place of failure, but also his restoration of the lost-and-found disciple after Easter, and the grail-question put to him: 'Simon, son of John, do you love me?' And Peter's response, 'Lord, you know everything; you know that I love you.' Jesus said to him, 'Feed my sheep'.[7]

I seem to see, secondly, the recognition scene in the garden early on Easter Day, when Mary Magdalene is looking for the body of Jesus. Here, too, is a cameo that is so sharply etched that I feel myself to be there, my feet wet with dew, my heart pounding with astonishment, wondering what can have happened in the darkness. 'Sir,' she says to the man in the garden, 'if you have carried him away, tell me where you have laid him.' The next verse in St John's Gospel is, I have no doubt in claiming, the hardest in the entire Bible to read aloud, effectively. 'Jesus said to her, *Mary!*'[8] How do you adequately catch the infinitely subtle nuances of that recognition, that Easter greeting? He calls her by name, by that most precious, most intimate possession of hers. At once, by the tone of the voice, the look in his eyes, the touch of his hand – how can we guess? – she knew him. 'Rabbonni!' she exclaims. Like Peter, I feel myself scanned in the garden, my past rushing up to meet me. But there is a difference. For Peter, recognition leads to tears. For Mary, it wipes them away. On Easter morning, I no longer want to run. On the contrary, as I see in the face of Christ the spark of resurrection, his eagerness to love, I know that the past – his Good Friday and mine – is put behind. I want to love him back, touch him, bind my life to his forever. I understand now that Easter is true, and that it will come true in my own life as Christ meets me and easters within me.

The final recognition I seem to see is the one that occurs a week later, behind shut doors, when Jesus comes to his disciples and stands among them and greets them with the Easter word of peace. I imagine him looking at Thomas the twin, who had said, 'Unless I see the mark of the nails in his hands, and put my finger in the mark of the nails and my hand in his side I will not believe.' Again, I find it hard to guess what passes between Jesus and Thomas at the moment of recognition: 'My Lord and my God!'⁹ But I know that there is a lot of myself in Thomas, a lot that finds religious faith stretching my credulity, wondering what has become of yesterday's bright dreams, fervent hopes and unrealised promises in the light of today's problems. I want to believe that there is something very loyal in Thomas' doubt, his unwillingness to he swept away on a wave of (as he sees it) hysteria. I want to believe that it is this very felt, religious quality of testing the truth that Jesus honours at the point of recognition. The marks of the nails are plain for me to see on the body of Christ in glory. Then as I return to the face that looks so resolutely at me out of its Easter light, if there is anything in me that deserves to be called faith, I feel Thomas's acclamation becoming mine, rising up out of somewhere deep inside me: 'My Lord and my God!' Despite everything, I can believe, and pray, 'Help my unbelief'.

THE HUMAN FACE OF GOD

Peter, Mary and Thomas: these recognition scenes are all part of my own recognition of Christ as I meet him in the tapestry. Failure, doubt and love are all experiences I know well. Somehow, I find that this Christ can contain and hold them. Our eyes meet. In him, I meet the human face of God. I encounter both his goodness and his severity (as St Paul puts it), but I encounter them in a form I can understand and respond to, incarnate in the person of Jesus. In him, I read God's complete commitment to the human race, to me. And as I recognise him, I know that the Easter destiny of Peter, of Mary and of Thomas, will be mine as well. God will make a worshipper out of me yet.

The human face of God. It is a lovely phrase. What I see on the tapestry is love incarnate, the Christ who is one of us, a loving, learning, suffering, triumphing human being, like us in all things, a contemporary who knows that 'joy and woe are

A PICTURE OF FAITH

woven fine'. His title on the great tapestry is 'Christ in Glory'. Yet I see him just as much a 'Man in glory'. He is, surely, the apotheosis of the tiny human figure between his feet. He is what that figure will become, by the grace of God; he is a picture of my glorious destiny.

A medieval mind would have found much to theologise upon the discovery that the centres of their two heads are exactly the same distance from the ends of the mandorla; in other words, the two foci of the womb, or the tomb, this ellipse of death and glory, are the man and the Man; everyman and archetypal Man; one man amongst others and the Man for others, particular and universal at the same time.[10] I see in the vast difference in scale between the two figures the truth that the grace of God, so to speak, expands me, enlarges me. It is the opposite of that diminishment into nothing that the devil at the side of the mandorla suggests. The Hebrew word for glory means 'weight', substantiality, solidity almost. My human, God-given destiny, says the gospel, is to become this enlarged, substantial, glorious figure. St John says that 'when he is revealed, we will be like him'.[11] St Paul promises that when all things come to fulfilment, in the age of 'the freedom of the glory of the children of God,' we will be 'conformed to the image of his Son, in order that he might be the first born within a large family,' and attain to the 'measure of the stature of the fullness of Christ'.[12]

It seems to me that the story of my life can be told as a process of both enlargement and diminishment: enlargement by love as I am drawn out of myself and into God and other people; diminishment by self concern as I am pulled into myself and contract towards nothing. It is tempting to say that there are experiences that enlarge and experiences that diminish. In one sense, that is true: when I am loved, or surrounded by beauty, or moved by another's compassion, there is the chance of enlargement. When I am hated, or bereaved, or in an ugly place, or witness to inhuman behaviour there is the possibility of diminishment. But as I write this, I know that there is a shorthand in this way of putting things. For in the face of life's ups and downs, the joys and woes that are woven fine, it is my choice and mine alone, as to whether I shall be enlarged or diminished through them. I can grow through the experience of ugliness; love may not automatically enlarge my soul.

'Happiness', said the preacher at our wedding one cold, windswept day high up in Wensleydale, 'is not a set of circumstances. It is a way of life.' He was elucidating the sixth chapter of Deuteronomy, with its great commandment of the Torah that we should love God with all our heart, soul, mind and strength. As I look back across the years to that day, I seem to hear him say that it is this divine gift of covenant love at work in our lives that makes for enlargement, in marriage as in all else, like the (to me) miracle of yeast causing dull, heavy dough to defy gravity and rise into something expansive, airy and wonderful. We all nowadays talk of personal 'growth'. It is an apt metaphor. The danger is that I think of it as inevitable as physical development, a relentless evolution of myself towards the perfect realisation of my potential. I have learned the hard way that it is not like that. I have to work for this growth, struggle to say 'yes' to love, make choices constantly between enlargement and diminishment; learn how to start again when my refusals, my 'no' have gained control, and I feel myself declining as a person away from that glorious stature of Christ.

It is a miracle of grace that I am not long left in that self-pitying, self-hating state of non-life. It is a terrible place to be. Like the prodigal in the parable, I come to my senses in time, realise that there is no fulfilment or satisfaction here, and begin to long for what I have lost. And so I start the long, hard climb back to reality, back home. Through prayer, the sacraments and scripture – the time-honoured 'means of grace' as we call them, for that is what they are; through the care of others, the gifts of beauty, laughter and the love of friends, through all the often lowly, insignificant signs of the goodness of God, I feel a stirring within me. The ice melts. Winter is over. I come alive once more. I begin, again, to grow.

The figure of Christ on the tapestry tells me that the measure of his stature, his fullness, is the gift of grace to me at the end of this road home. But it tells me something else too. For I seem to see him in the act of standing up, arms raised in greeting his runaway child, just like the loving father who, says the parable, when he saw his son coming home, went running to meet him.[13]

FATHER AND MOTHER

Like the loving father, I said, for he is the parent who features in the parable. Recently at a workshop for lay people, I invited participants to role-play the parable. I allocated the parts of the father, the two brothers and the servant. 'What about the fatted calf?' asked somebody frivolously. But there was an important omission, of course – the mother of the two sons, who is not even hinted at in the story. I decided to write her in, allocated the part, and sat back to watch what would happen. It was most illuminating. In the half hour or so we gave to the exercise, the delicate dynamics of the parable shifted noticeably. The presence of the mother seemed to push the father into a more traditionally masculine stance. It was as if the father's tenderness, his compassion, his vulnerability towards his sons passed to the mother instead; while he stepped back somewhat, began to look on things more dispassionately and take on the traditional, patriarchal role of arbiter and judge. In other words, the mother took over those gentle, feminine, feeling qualities which are so lovely a part of the father's personality, while he reverted to a male stereotype of fatherhood.

By contrast, Christ on the tapestry is no male stereotype.[14] This is no patriarchal Lord. Man he is, the archetypal, noble human figure, in whom the presence of God shines out; Man, but not so much a man, for there is a strong sense of the feminine in him, of the maternal. The limitations of language and the need to ascribe gender to pronouns make it hard to put into words. There is a beard, it is true, and a man's face (though with infinite compassion in its still strength). But the role suggests 'her' as much as 'him', the way the mandorla's womblike ellipse is powerfully reflected in the oval of the lower part of the figure, as well as in the folds around the elbows, and the shape of the face itself. Some people speak disparagingly about the belly of a wasp. For me, this aspect of the figure is so deliberate a feature of this Christ that I want to stay with it and see if I can grasp a meaning here.

I think I glimpse an answer in that role play of the parable, where I learned that in the portrayal of the father, there is a perfect equilibrium between masculine and feminine. Indeed, it is not so much that he is father as parent, showing the integration in one human person of both fatherly and motherly qualities. 'Good enough' parenting,[15] the psychoanalysts tell us, means a 'good enough' exposure to fatherliness and motherliness, normally (but not necessarily) embodied in a biological father and mother. The loving parent of the prodigal is an ideal figure embodying both, it seems to me, and that is how I see Christ too: as the one whose face proclaims him to be father, and whose robe mother; the fountain of light and life through whom all is created, but also the womb of love in whom all is nurtured and cherished. The word 'androgynous' feels too analytical to do justice to this sensitive balance of male-female energies the tapestry depicts. Two great writers of our Christian spiritual tradition come closer to it. It was a renaissance man, St Francis de Sales, who said: 'Nothing is so strong as gentleness; and nothing is so loving and gentle as strength.' It was a medieval woman, Mother Julian of Norwich, who dared to exclaim that Jesus Christ 'is both our father and our mother'. So as I contemplate him, I begin to hear the different nuances in those invitations in the gospel to find rest and shelter and peace. I can come to Christ as mother as well as father. I can see in Christ the womb that bore me. I can know myself held, caressed, embraced and fed. I understand how 'love was his meaning'. And that is 'good enough' for time and for eternity.

AN ETERNAL WEIGHT OF GLORY

And eternity is almost the final word in my meditation. The perspectives shift again. I see Christ seated now, enthroned in glory. Around him, the mandorla has expanded into infinite space: the deep indigo becomes a sky that seems to contain an entire universe of which he is Pantocrator, king and lord. The tapestry says to me that he is a cosmic, universal Christ, the Christ who, in the words of the Letter to the Ephesians, 'is the same one who ascended far above all the heavens, so that he might fill all things'.[16] And this filling of all things, as he fills the mandorla, is the continuation of his work of creation and redemption, the bringing about of God's wise and loving purposes. He 'sustains all things by his powerful word',[17] says the opening of the Letter to the Hebrews, that great celebration of the ascended Son of God. And what is that affirmation that he 'sustains', or 'bears along' all that is, but that he is the ground of all being, the personal expression of the love that moves the sun and the other stars, the Christ in whom the centre holds.

Seated amid the galaxies, the tapestry depicts . . . a human being. I gaze into the eye of the universe, and seem to hear ringing round the cosmos the words of Pontius Pilate: 'Behold the man!'[18] Theologians speak about the taking of our humanity into God in the second Person of the Trinity. It is a rich phrase. But when I contemplate this man of the cosmos, it is as if the words run out. I am silenced by this form of a servant among the constellations, his simple robe, the blood on his hands and feet. The architect of the universe might still be the ordinary craftsman, his hands wielding their tools in the carpenter's workshop of Nazareth. In this cosmic Christ, I see the humility of God, the same servant-humility that the world saw when Pilate brought Jesus out before the people, wearing the crown of thorns and the purple robe.

Outside, across the ruins of the old Cathedral, is Jacob Epstein's great sculpture of Christ before Pilate, 'Ecce Homo'. It is massive, elemental, archaic, the bent figure barely emerging from the hunk of rock from which it is cut, like some stone-age figure struggling out of a cave. These two Christs gaze at each other through the glass screen at the west end of the Cathedral: a humiliated Christ and a regal, exalted Christ; the man of the earth and the man of heaven; a figure of sorrow and a figure of joy. Yet as I stand between them, and realise that my entire life is lived between these two symbols of passion and resurrection, joy and woe, I see that they are not two Christs, but one. He is the primal man of stone as well as sky, victor in death as well as in life, the wounded king of all who bear the mark of pain.

These words *Ecce homo*, behold the man, I believe, make it possible for me to pray. For they offer me an image, an icon of flesh and blood, for me to focus on as I peer into the indigo sky and call out into the void to see if there is anyone there. This cosmic Christ is attired, says the artist, in a priest's robe,[19] as if bearing our human condition into the very heart of God. 'Yet he loves the earth he leaves,' says Wesley's Ascension Day hymn – or perhaps leaves only in order not to leave it, only in order to fill all things, fill the earth with that 'pure unbounded love' that is himself. I find I can pray, for I can sense that I am not alone in this void, because there is a presence, a consciousness, a personal energy that has reached out and touched mine in Jesus, made contact with it, has 'become like his brothers and sisters in every respect,' and now fills creation, 'crowned with glory and honour'[20] as the picture language of the New Testament puts it. The Letter to the Hebrews says that he is 'a merciful and faithful high priest in the service of God', one who stands for me and identifies forever with my own wounds, my own weaknesses, my own fear: 'Because he himself was tested by what he suffered, he is able to help those who are being tested.'[21]

For me, a human being, this cosmic human figure with compassion in his face says to me that at the core of an indifferent, even cruel universe, there is a personal presence, a kindness, a love. I see this love in the form in which he and she has touched me, a human figure. As I look into the universe, and consider that the light from the stars I see will have taken light years to reach me, that what I am seeing is the universe's distant past, I speculate whether this love at its core has manifested itself in other ways to other beings, touched remote galaxies and been 'made flesh' in forms I could scarcely guess at. As I look at the tapestry, a poem of Alice Meynell comes to mind:

Nor, in our little day,
May his devices with the heavens be guessed,

171

His pilgrimage to thread the Milky Way,
Or his bestowals there be manifest.

But, in the eternities,
Doubtless we shall compare together, hear
A million alien Gospels, in what guise
He trod the Pleiades, the Lyre, the Bear.

O be prepared, my soul!
To read the inconceivable, to scan
The million forms of God those stars unroll,
When, in our turn, we show to them a Man.[22]

The question is unanswerable; yet it keeps me humble in the presence of deep majesty. Perhaps the four mythical creatures of fantasy hint at this, suggest that the cosmic Christ reaches out to the elusive stuff of this and other universes in ways beyond imagining: grace completing and crowning nature in an infinitely marvellous variety of ways. For us, the acclamation is 'Behold the man!' Cosmologists talk about the 'anthropic principle', that the universe is somehow the way it is because there are evolved, conscious beings, ourselves, to observe it.[23] Mystical contemplation of the tapestry asks me a kind of cosmic grail question: if Christ is this universal presence, this force of compassion holding the centre of things, then would we not expect to encounter him, as the poem says, in a million alien guises, each one a particular, unique incarnation of the love of God?

Once again, it is the sky that puts me in my place. It reawakens faith that love, in its fragile, vulnerable way, wins through in the end. Teilhard de Chardin spoke of the 'Omega point', that point of consummation when heaven and earth are finally enfolded in a single piece, the purposes of love have been achieved, and the cosmos is finally reconciled. The tapestry is an icon of hope as I struggle and work for the coming of God's kingdom, as I wait for this Omega Christ who is the end of all life and existence, the love who is all in all.

I sense that the world is already on its long march home, that loving hands are already raised in greeting:

> We shall rest and see,
> We shall see and love,
> We shall love and praise.
> Behold what shall be in the end without end!
> For what other thing is our end but to come to that
>   kingdom of which there is no end![24]

Part Three

MOVING OUT AGAIN

'When you look again at the tapestry forget, as far as you can, everything that we have said. Perhaps there is another life in it altogether, another, different meaning. Fix nothing. Throw away everything you already understand. Otherwise the tapestry will die for you and you will not see it any more, only your ideas about it . . . If anyone points out the moon to you and you see it, do you go on staring at the finger?'

Andrew Harvey, *A Journey in Ladakh*

16

THE SIGNATURE

COMING DOWN AGAIN

TO REACH the centre feels like reaching the end of the journey. There is that sense that I have arrived at a longed-for destination. I see what I came to see; and like the Queen of Sheba, travelling those hundreds of hot dusty miles to visit Solomon in all his glory, I too acknowledge that the half was never told me. I could not have guessed that this journey into the fibres of a tapestry would turn out to illuminate so much of life.

I said at the outset that I was thinking of this book as a personal *Baedeker*. The itinerary, the views that compel my attention, the places I choose to stop to admire the landscape – these are all very much my own, personal voyage. I began my meditation by seeing the tapestry from afar off, like the mountains I recall seeing from afar as a child. I now feel myself to be in the position of a sherpa escorting people across these mountains. Look over here, I want to say; look there: do you see what I see? Not, see it *as* I see it, but see it in your own way, and let our ways of seeing mutually enrich one another.

The time comes, however, when we must leave the mountains and return to life on the plain. It is important *how* we do that. Taking leave of the tapestry, turning away from the face of Christ, is like saying farewell to a friend. You do it gently, and with love. Jerk your head away and you risk fracturing the delicate gift of intimacy. Conversely, the more attention I give to someone or something, the more care I shall find myself taking over the all-important task of saying good-bye.

This is certainly true of life's richer, more intense, moments: the 'peak experiences' we call them, to echo the metaphor of mountains. Body and soul need time both to enter and leave these high places. Peter Matthieson, in his book

The Snow Leopard, talks about 'coming down' at the end of a Himalayan journey:

> I remembered how careful one must be not to talk too much, or move abruptly, after a silent week of Zen retreat . . . It is crucial to emerge gradually from such a chrysalis, drying our wings in the sun's quiet, like a butterfly, to avoid a sudden tearing of the spirit.[1]

Sometimes, at the altar rail, I am quite taken aback by the abruptness with which people sometimes push the chalice away when they have received, get up and turn their back almost callously on the sacrament that offers them life and healing. When you visit the Sikh temple, the *Gurdwara* (and how hospitable the Sikhs are to those who are not of their faith), the first thing you are told is how the Sikhs reverence their scriptures, the *Adi Granth*. The greatest insult you can pay a Sikh is to turn your back on their holy book. So you walk backwards out of the temple, rather as old-fashioned etiquette demanded that you took your leave of the sovereign.

And perhaps, in all kinds of other ways, how we 'take leave' of people and things tells of the reverence, or lack of it, with which we hold life, hold the God who meets us there.

I remember, for example, going to the Egyptian Museum in Berlin to see the head of Nefertite. I cannot say that I went in with much more in mind than ticking it off my list: there were things the visitor *ought* to see in Berlin and this was one of them. I joined a crowd of schoolchildren, listened non-commitally to what their teacher was saying, read the information by the display case. Then, duty done, I turned rather too decisively away and headed off towards the exit. On reaching the street, however, something stopped me and called me back. It suddenly dawned on me that I had turned my back, without a second thought, on one of the greatest art-treasures antiquity had bequeathed us. Far from saying farewell to it, I had not even greeted it or seen it for what it was. I went back into the museum where, now, that incredibly beautiful head seemed to illuminate the darkness of the room it occupied. And then, when it was time to go, I was more careful about how I turned away.

A DIFFERENT EYE

'When an image enters your heart and establishes itself, you flee in vain: the image will remain with you.' So a 13th century Persian writer imagines Gabriel addressing Mary.[2] That is how I want to take leave of the tapestry: taking its images with me, in the hope that they will, like Nefertite, illumine the darkness a little and make a difference to how I view things. How might that happen?

It has to happen within me. That is the first thing to say. Nothing on the tapestry can compel me to take its image with me. It is my choice whether I do so or not. This is true of any of those 'peak experiences' I have talked about, whether they are once-in-a-lifetime Himalayan adventures, or the more ordinary, yet still God-filled, encounters of every day. It comes down to attitude. I can be a kind of spiritual sightseer, logging up 'experiences', doing what is expected of the keen religious man or woman, yet never really changed by any of it, never opened up to God in a new way, never deepened in myself. That would be the equivalent of how I went into the Berlin museum. Again, the eucharist provides us with an appalling metaphor. I can hold out my hands and receive the body of Christ. But this greatest of all symbolic acts, taking Christ into my very self, ingesting his presence, merging with him, *may make no difference to me at all.* I may 'die with a head full of fine sayings and a perfectly empty heart'.[3] The signs may all be there, but not the thing signified. Like the cross, the eucharist is not coercive truth.

Perhaps, however, instead of being a sightseer, I can become a sight*seer*, that is someone who sees, as well as looks. I have talked about the tapestry as an icon that draws me into its window, makes a contemplative out of me. And that, I think, is what I am looking for: a way of seeing that can become a way of worshipping and a way of being. There is a story about a Zen master who attained enlightenment. This is what he said to

Sutherland · MCMLXII ·

PINTON ℞ FELLETIN

celebrate it: 'Oh wondrous marvel! I chop wood! I draw water from the well!' Anthony de Mello, who quotes this story, says that 'after enlightenment, nothing really changes, the tree is still a tree; people are just what they were before and so are you . . . The one difference is that you see things with a different eye.'[4]

The essence of contemplation, he says, is 'the sense of wonder'. And wonder, he goes on, does not take me out of the real world where there is wood to be chopped and water to be drawn. On the contrary, the work of contemplation, its 'heart work', is not different from the work of living, the work that fills most of out waking lives. It is not different from it, but it does transform it. I see it with a different eye. And that is what I need more than anything else, some new, God-orientated way of living, so that I come to see the whole of life as pure gift, to be celebrated and truly *lived*.

I call this living *eucharistically*, because *eucharistia*, 'thanksgiving', lies at the heart of the authentic Christian life. To celebrate the eucharist is, in a profound way, to learn how to celebrate life, to discover how the whole of life can become worship, our 'reasonable sacrifice' St Paul calls it.[5] He speaks of 'being transformed', literally, about the 'metamorphosis' of life, just as the natural things of the eucharist, bread and wine, are metamorphosed, given back to us in a new way. It is no new insight, but still a thought-provoking one, that the Christian vocation is the same as the vocation of the communion bread: to be taken, blessed, broken, and given – given, that is, to the world as living signs of Christ's presence. Modern eucharistic theology teaches us that it is not the 'words of consecration' alone, but rather the entire act of thanksgiving, 'saying the blessing', that effects this transformation. This seems to me to be a symbol of what is true of all of life, that saying 'thank you' changes things, changes *me*, gives me a 'different eye'. We bless God, and the world is redeemed.

TAKING LEAVE OF GOD

At the beginning of this book, I talked about the two fundamental movements of life: *upward* and *inward*. All of religion, all of life is in those movements, I suggested. I should, perhaps, have included this third movement I am faced with now, the movement *outward*. For religion is nothing if it is not connected with the world, if God is not a God of the ordinary and the workaday. In reality, I don't believe that this movement outward is different from the movements inward and upward. As I learn to love God, I learn to love my neighbour also. If I were to move upward and inward, hut not outward at the same time, I would not in fact be making any sort of worthwhile journey at all. It would be no more than escapism into a fantasy world that may offer the illusion of making me feel better (for a time), but changes nothing and nobody, least of all myself.

The medieval German mystic Meister Eckhart wrote: 'Man's best and highest moment is when he takes his leave of God.' I have thought often about those words, and what they could mean. Probably he means that the highest spiritual state a person can attain is when he or she abandons images of 'God', and surrenders to his pure Being. In that sense, the tapestry can never be an end in itself. There will come a time when we need to lay aside its images, or perhaps be led *through* them up into the 'high window' where his dwelling place, metaphorically speaking, is.

But equally, his words can be taken in the sense that there is a right, God-given autonomy I need to discover when I am living and working 'in the world'; that being a human being means to live, very often, in Bonhoeffer's phrase, *etsi deus non daretur*, as if God were not a given fact of life. 'The God who lets us live in the world without the working hypothesis of God is the God before whom we stand continually. Before God and with God, we live without God.'[6] Perhaps the most religious way of living in a world come of age, Bonhoeffer tells me, is to be as human as I can, not intensely preoccupied with God every moment of the day but, having committed my life to him in worship and prayer, being content to leave it at that, and relax.

So how do I take leave of the vision of God, move out from that encounter, re-enter the ordinary human world, yet without losing that 'different eye' that makes all the difference between mere existence and the joyous privilege of *living*? I look on the tapestry for some clue, some symbol that will help me make this all-important connection between worship and work, between contemplative prayer and active involvement.

THE SIGNATURE

It came to me very late on that there was such a clue. It was as I was pondering the liturgy – a tapestry of actions and texts that, like the Great Tapestry, has its own warp and weft that contain Christ in Glory. In the eucharist, it is a few small words that enable us to turn away from worship and embrace once more the world of work; or, you could say, more evocatively, to turn away from Christ in order to embrace him in a different place and with a different face. This colophon is, of course, the dismissal: 'Go in peace to love and serve the Lord'. In the Latin rite, the very name of the liturgy is derived from the word of dismissal: 'ite, missa est'. It is as if these concluding words are the signature of the mass, these words that thrust us out of liturgy and into life.

The tapestry too has its signature. There is writing floating in the sea of green; words that come as something of a surprise when the tapestry's language is so visual. There are words and words, of course: words you hear, speak and read; and other words that you see and touch and handle: a wedding ring, a glass of water on a hot day, the embrace of lover or friend. The sacraments are like this, pledges of God's love for us. St Augustine called the sacraments God's 'visible words', for they go beyond what spoken words can do. They touch the senses, fill out meanings, make incarnate. I see the tapestry as a 'visible word', or rather a visible book. And what I have written has been no more than written words laid at the foot of visible ones.

So, when I come across a written text, however brief, placed prominently in an environment that is so visual and so invested with symbolic meaning, I am bound to ask the question, why? What are these words saying to me? Do they too have a symbolic function of some kind? Or are they simply islands of prose in an ocean of art and poetry?

The signature anchors the tapestry into its particular historical context. It tells us the name of the artist, SUTHERLAND, the weavers, PINTON, the place where it was made, FELLETIN, and the date of its public unveiling, MCMLXII. It announces the facts that belong to the tapestry's making. It documents it and establishes its credentials. I know where this work of art has come from, for the words tell the story.

But there is more to this, I sense, than the documentation of a great work of art. I smile at the portrayal of the Queen in Alan Bennet's play *A Question of Attribution*, where monarch and art historian come face to face in the royal collection. 'Facts,' she demands, 'feed me facts': an incongruous request in the contemplative, image-centred world of an art gallery, where symbols, meanings and interpretations are all. I doubt, then, whether *mere* facts belong on the tapestry either; or put it this way, I suspect that words framed by such immense, powerful images are bound themselves to take on a symbolic life of their own.

As I read the names that I am collectively calling the tapestry's signature, I think of the words of Elgar at the end of his score of *The Dream of Gerontius*, 'this is the best of me.' It is as if I am being asked, or perhaps God is, to accept and to celebrate the best of the artist, the best of those who collaborated with him. And it is the best achievement of human minds and skills and hands. The tapestry is no miracle. It is the outcome of years of effort, of difficulty even, of struggle. Poised on either side of the crucified Jesus, I almost see in these names some such statement as: 'this is my body', 'this is my blood'. Art is very much about giving up body and blood: it does not come without price. The names on the tapestry recall to me the human beings for whom its creation was *work*. It is not to demean their achievement to hazard the guess that there must have been times when it seemed just a 'job', with perhaps its own share of unexciting routine. All creative work (in other words, all work) is like that. To my mind, there is a true dignity in doing a 'job' well, giving myself to it without holding anything back, body and blood. There is a 'worth' here that is akin, etymologically and theologically, to 'worship'. Warp and weft are all one.

I wonder if I would see the tapestry in quite the same way if it were not for this signature. I see a parallel here with some of the letters of St Paul. At the end of the First Letter to the Corinthians, and again at the end of Galatians, we suddenly come across the apostle's signature: 'I, Paul, write this greeting with my own hand';[6] 'See what large letters I make when I am writing with my own hand.'[7] This, following chapter after chapter of some of the toughest theological argument in the New Testament, is an unlooked-for sign of humanity. It is as if the human hands of the writer insist on declaring themselves, making it plain that whatever we mean by the inspiration, the 'God-breathedness', of the scriptures, it is never a process that bypasses human ingenuity, struggle and skill. St Paul's signature locates his writings in the canon of human literature as well as the canon of the Bible. It reassures me that his letters have their own *Sitz im Leben*, a setting in a life that is as real and experienced as my own. I need to know that he shares my body and blood, if his writings are to be of any use to me.

So the signature on the tapestry recalls my own hands to me, hands that are symbols of my endeavour, my achievement, my failure and my very life. 'Christ has no hands but your hands' said Teresa of Avila, herself no stranger to the stresses placed upon a person when God calls to the creative life of soul-making. The signature gives me the clue I need when I ask how I can take the image with me, see life with this 'different eye'. I see, in those names and in that place and date, my own nature and name: the person God has made me, the people he has set me amongst, the place and time in history to which he calls me to belong. My contemplation of the tapestry leads me back, full circle, to the contemplation of my own hands and, from there, to the world those hands were made to serve.

These few words in an immensity of symbols, then, are for me like the dismissal at the end of the eucharist. They are an invitation, no, a summons, to make concrete what I have glimpsed of Christ in Glory, to enable him to do his work through whatever it is I have to offer. The signature is a demonstration of commitment and of love. I sign my name to what I believe in, am committed to. Early on in this book,

I spoke about the life task of becoming artists of our own lives. So, what I am now saying is that I must put my name to the picture I am making, own it as mine by my signature. To do that means asking how much love is going into the fashioning of this work of art that is me, how far I can say of myself, 'This is the best of me'.

THE BRIDGE IS LOVE

One of the most remarkable pieces of writing to emerge out of the Jewish holocaust was Viktor Frankl's book *Man's Search for Meaning*. His experience of concentration camp existence taught him that 'he who has a *why* to live can bear with almost any *how*'. In his book, Frankl describes how he took with him to Auschwitz the manuscript of his first book, hidden in his coat. It did not survive. For him, it was this destruction of his spiritual child that first posed the question whether his life ultimately possessed any meaning at all.

> Not yet did I notice that an answer to this question with which I was wrestling so passionately was already in store for me . . . I had to surrender my clothes, and in turn inherited the worn-out rags of an inmate who had already been sent to the gas-chamber . . . Instead of the many pages of my manuscript, I found in a pocket of the newly acquired coat one single page torn out of a Hebrew prayer hook, containing the main Jewish prayer, *Shema Israel*. How should I have interpreted such a 'coincidence' other than as a challenge to live my thoughts, instead of merely putting them on paper?[9]

Shema Israel: the command ringing out across the centuries when a desert God summoned a people to be his. 'Hear, O Israel, the Lord is our God, the Lord alone. You shall love the Lord your God with all your heart, and with all your soul, and with all your might.'[10] I too must learn to do more than think my thoughts. I must learn to live them, make them body and blood through the hands God gives me. 'Preach the gospel everywhere' said St Francis of Assisi. 'Use words if necessary.'

The Bridge of San Luis Rey is Thornton Wilder's great novel about a disaster in eighteenth century Peru, when the eponymous bridge collapses, without warning, precipitating five travellers into the abyss below. Juniper, a Franciscan brother, tries to make sense of the tragedy by studying the careers of the five victims in an attempt to show that the 'accident' was really the outcome of causes hidden deep within the personalities of the victims, as well as within the mind of God himself. The novel tells the stories of the five unfortunates. Needless to say, Juniper's attempt at theodicy, justifying the ways of God to mortals, fails. But the book ends with Juniper's profound insight. 'The bridge' he says 'is love, the only survival, the only meaning.'[11]

And there is the passageway I need to take my leave of the tapestry. The bridge is love: this movement of love that flows out of Christ in Glory into the whole cosmos; that flows towards every creature and every human soul; that flows through those whose hearts have been touched by the goodness of God into the places of struggle and suffering and pain. 'The bridge is love': I can be that bridge, that point of connection to enable heaven and earth to touch.

I turn from the tapestry and know what is required of me.

CHAPTER 1: FROM FAR OFF

1. The many changes undergone by the design during that time are chronicled in *Christ in Glory in the Tetramorph: The Genesis of the Great Tapestry in Coventry Cathedral* by Graham Sutherland and Andrew Revai (London, 1964). This book is hereafter cited as *CT*. Not only does this study offer a fascinating insight into the developing relationship between an artist and his subject; it also provides an invaluable guide to the interpretation of the tapestry in its own right, and I am deeply indebted to it in my own work.
2. *CT* 84-87.
3. *Revelations of Divine Love*, chapter 56 (in the edition by Grace Warrack, London, 1952), 135.
4. See, for example, Henri J. M. Nouwen's meditation on a Rembrandt canvas in his *The Return of the Prodigal Son*, 1992.
5. *CT* 11, from the introduction by Eric Newton.
6. Matthew 6:6. Unless otherwise indicated, biblical quotations are from the *New Revised Standard Version of the Bible* (New York and Oxford, 1989).
7. *CT*, 79.

CHAPTER 2: A MAGIC CARPET

1. Robert Holdstock, *Mythago Wood* (London, 1987), 9.
2. The phrase belongs to the title of Gerard Hughes' book *God of Surprises* (London, 1985).
3. Blaise Pascal, *Pensées* (translated A. J. Krailsheimer, Harmondsworth, 1966), 36.
4. More exactly, 'Everything begins as a *mystique* and ends as a *politique*'. See Alan Ecclestone, *A Staircase for Silence* (London, 1977), 84ff. for a discussion of Péguy's famous dictum.
5. 2 Corinthians 3:18.
6. Søren Kierkegaard, *Purity of Heart is to Will One Thing*, translated by Douglas Steere (London, 1961).
7. *CT*, 32.
8. Ruth Page, *Ambiguity and the Presence of God* (London, 1985), 13. She speaks about ambiguity as 'multivalent'.
9. The allusion is to William Blake's *Auguries of Innocence*. The passage is quoted in chapter 6.

CHAPTER 3: TRAVELLING COMPANIONS

1. Matthew Arnold, The Future in *Poems* (London, 1930), 195.
2. Walt Whitman, 'Passage to India' in *Leaves of Grass* (New York, n.d.), 329.
3. Philip Toynbee, *End of a Journey: An Autobiographical Journal 1979-1981* (London, 1988), 330.
4. Michael Sadgrove, 'Companions of Christ', *Theology XCVI* (1993), 128ff.
5. See Dante's *The Divine Comedy* in the translation by Dorothy L Sayers (Harmondsworth, 1949).
6. *Inferno*, Canto l; *The Divine Comedy*: Hell, 71.
7. Thus, for example: 'Much of theology before, during and after the war lacked the qualities of ambivalence, paradox, irony, tragedy, grief, sophistication, which are necessary to cope with the complexity of experience. The poet sometimes seemed abler to cope with ambivalence than the theologian.' So Alan Wilkinson, *The Church of England and the First World War* (London, 1978), 244.
8. *CT*, 80.
9. *Paradiso*, Canto 33: *The Divine Comedy*: Paradise, 347.
10. Emily Dickinson, *The Complete Poems* (London, 1975), 327.
11. Ecclesiasticus 38:34.
12. Vita Sackville-West, 'Craftsmen' in Philip Larkin, ed., *The Oxford Book of Twentieth Century Verse* (Oxford, 1973), 269.
13. The personal motto of John Henry Newman: 'heart speaks to heart'.
14. *Pensées*, 154.

CHAPTER 4: ICON: IMAGE AND PRESENCE

1. Mark 10:46-52.
2. Izaak Walton, *Life of George Herbert*, 1674 in *Works of George Herbert* (London, n.d.), 24.
3. George Herbert, 'The Elixir', in *Works of George Herbert*, 250.
4. Samuel Johnson, *The History of Rasselas*, cited Anthony storr, *Solitude* (London, 1989), 64.
5. George Herbert, 'The Pulley', in *Works of George Herbert*, 221.
6. 'Proslogion' in *The Prayers and Meditations of St Anselm* ed. Benedicta Ward (Harmondsworth, 1973), 238. It is worth noting the entire discussion is couched in the context of a prayer.
7. Mark 1:10,11.
8. Mark 15:38.
9. Revelation 2:17. Jung speaks extensively about 'soul-stones' as a common human phenomenon, where the stone symbolised the 'self': e.g. C. J. Jung, *Memories, Dreams, Reflections* (London, 1993), 38, 42. I am grateful to Tony Bryer for this illuminating comment on the symbolism of Revelation.
10. Luke 2:41-51.
11. Colossians 3:3.
12. Colossians 1:27.
13. Job 42:5.
14. Psalm 8:3,4.
15. William Wordsworth, 'Lines Composed a Few Miles Above Tintern Abbey' in *Poetical Works* (London, n.d.), 175.
16. Colossians 1:15.

CHAPTER 5: WOVEN FINE

1. Unpublished paper, *The Coventry Tapestry Weavers* by Joan Browne, n.d.
2. Romans 8:28.
3. W. H. Auden, 'Musée des Beaux Arts' in *Selected Poems* (London, 1979), 79.
4. John 19:24,25.
5. 'Auguries of Innocence', lines 56-60, in *Complete Writings*, the edition by Geoffrey Keynes (Oxford, 1966), 432.
6. Cited by Keith Botsford in an article in *The Independent* on 'Lent', 23 Feb 1991.
7. Matthew 2:16-18.
8. T. S. Eliot, 'Burnt Norton' in *Collected Poems 1909-1962* (London, 1974), 190.
9. Carole King, *Tapestry*.
10. William Blake, *Auguries of Innocence*.
11. Philip Larkin, 'Days' in *Collected Poems* (London, 1988), 67.
12. Hebrews 3:15, quoting the *Venite*, Psalm 95.
13. Letter to Lady Georgiana Morpeth, 16 February 1820; quoted in Alan Bell, *Sydney Smith: A Biography* (Oxford, 1980), 138.
14. J. P. de Caussade, *Self Abandonment to Divine Providence* (in the translation by A. Thorold) (Glasgow, 1974), 33, 68ff.
15. Matthew 6:34.
16. Søren Kierkegaard, *Journals*, the edition by Alexander Dru (London, 1958), 89.
17. 1 Corinthians 13:12.
18. Gerard Manley Hopkins, 'The Wreck of the Deutschland', *Poems*, edited by Robert Bridges (Oxford, 1933), 13.

CHAPTER 6: COAT OF MANY COLOURS

1. The coat Joseph's father Jacob made for him is traditionally rendered as a 'coat of many colours' (Genesis 37:3). The meaning of the Hebrew is uncertain here, but a more likely understanding

is that it was a 'long robe with sleeves'. However, the 'many colours' have passed so thoroughly into the folklore both ancient and modern (e.g. the musical by Tim Rice and Andrew Lloyd-Webber, *Joseph and the Amazing Technicolour Dreamcoat*) that I need not apologise for alluding to it here.

2. Nikolaus Pevsner and Alexandra Wedgwood, *The Buildings of England: Warwickshire* (Harmondsworth, 1966), 256.

3. Genesis 1:31.

4. William Blake *Auguries of Innocence,* lines 1-4, 431.

5. John Milton, 'At a Solemn Musick', *Poetical Works* in the edition by H. C. Beeching (London, 1906), line 23, 16.

6. Oxyrynchus Papyrus, cited in Esther de Waal, *Seeking God* (London, 1984), 112.

7. Peter Matthieson, *The Snow Leopard* (London, 1980), 212-3.

8. *Creation Festival Liturgy* (WWF and the International Consultancy on Religion, Education and Culture, 1988). The words are by Martin Palmer.

9. William Blake, *Auguries of Innocence*, 431.

10. Julian of Norwich, *Revelations of Divine Love*, Chapter 5, 10.

11. T. C. McLuhan, ed., *Touch the Earth: A Self-Portrait of Indian Existence* (London, 1973), 8. These were the words of Young Chief, of the Cayuse Indians, on signing away the Indians' land to the Americans in 1855.

12. Lawrence Binyon, 'The Burning of the Leaves' in *Oxford Book of Twentieth Century English Verse*, 102.

13. Revelation 21:1.

CHAPTER 7: BEAUTY AND THE BANDS

1. Quoted in Laurens van der Post, *Jung and the Story of Our Time* (Harmondsworth, 1978), 187.

2. *CT*, 29. Sutherland describes how he was fascinated by the 'burial bands' of early Egyptian and Graeco-Roman funeral art. These are the tapes which bind the portraits to their coffins.

3. Genesis 1:2. The Hebrew phrase recurs only once in the Old Testament, at Jeremiah 4:23, where it announces an oracle of disintegration.

4. 1 Kings 4:33,34.

5. Proverbs 6:6.

6. Psalm 1:4.

7. Mark 4:35-41.

8. Mark 5:1-20.

9. Romans 6:4.

10. *Institutes of the Christian Religion* I,6, in the translation by Henry Beveridge (London, 1962), 64.

11. Mark 8:24.

12. G. K. Chesterton, cited by Dennis Healey, *The Time of My Life* (London, 1989), 14.

13. *The Rule of St Benedict*, translated by O Hunter Blair (Fort Augustus, 1948), chapter 73, 181.

14. *The Rule of St Benedict* Prologue, 11.

15. Zechariah 11:7 (AV).

16. This, rather than the pursuit of solitude or retreat for its own sake. See Bede, *History of the English Church and People*, translated by Leo Sherley-Price, revised by R. E. Latham (Harmondsworth, 1968), 261.

17. 'It becomes more and more evident as one reads his [Sutherland's] account of endless experiments made and abandoned that the struggle was a real and exhausting one . . . I can remember no other account of a struggle of this kind in which an artist has deliberately flirted with his own temptations, actually making endless diagrams, quotations as it were from the past only in order to reject them, as a boxer might study his opponent's technique of attack in order to develop his own line of defence.' *CT*, 15.

18. R. S. Thomas, 'Poetry for Supper' in his *Selected Poems 1946-1968* (1986), 53.

19. 1 Corinthians 9:24-27.

20. In his poem 'Prayer', in *Works of George Herbert,* 97.
21. William Blake, 'Jerusalem' in *Complete Writings,* 716.
22. *The Wit and Wisdom of the Christian Fathers of Egypt,* translated by E. A. Wallis Budge (Oxford, 1934), 88.

CHAPTER 8: THE HIGH WINDOW: THE LIGHT AND THE DOVE
1. John Dunne, *House of Wisdom* (London, 1985), 113.
2. G. Alexinski, *Slavonic Mythology* in *New Larousse Encyclopaedia of Mythology* (London, 1968), 283.
3. Philip Larkin, 'High Windows' in *Collected Poems,* 165.
4. *CT,* 91.
5. Isaiah 64:5,7.
6. Ludwig Wittengenstein, *Tractatus* (London, 1961), 7.
7. F. W. Robertson, 'The Scepticism of Pilate' in *Sermons, First Series* (London, 1903), 300. The text for the sermon was John 18:38: 'What is truth?'
8. Psalm 139:1.
9. Genesis 1:2.
10. John 1:1-14.
11. *Gandhi: An Autobiography* (London, 1966), 94.
12. Matthew Arnold, 'The Buried Life', in *Poems,* 168.
13. Helen Gardner, ed., *The Metaphysical Poets* (Harmondsworth, 1973), 169.
14. Marcel Proust, *A la Recherche du Temps Perdu,* translated by C.K. Scott-Moncrieff and T. Kilmartin as *Remembrance of Things Past* (London, 1983), I, 73.
15. 1 John 1:7.
16. T. S. Eliot, 'Little Gidding', *Four Quartets* in *Collected Poems 1909-1962* (London, 1974), 221.

CHAPTER 9: THE VIOLENCE BENEATH: THE CRUCIFIXION
1. Elizabeth Jennings, 'The Shaking World' in *Collected Poems* (Manchester, 1987), 96.
2. Matthew 27:51.
3. See, for example, Edward C. Whitmont, *Return of the Goddess* (London, 1987).
4. Psalm 74:14-17; Psalm 89:10.
5. Mark 15:33.
6. Hebrews 9:27 (AV).
7. Philip Larkin, 'Aubade', in *Collected Poems,* 208.
8. Elie Wiesel, *The Fifth son* (Harmondsworth, 1987), 19.
9. The words of Querry in Graham Greene, *A Burnt-Out Case* (London, 1962), 287.
10. 1 Corinthians 1:18ff.
11. Isaiah 53:5 (AV).
12. See, on this, W. H. Vanstone, *Love's Endeavour, Love's Expense* (London, 1977).
13. V. Gollancz, *A Year of Grace* (Harmondsworth, 1955), 209.
14. John 12:32. Some Greek manuscripts read 'all things', a rendering that strengthens this important saying even further.
15. F. Dostoevsky, *The Brothers Karamazov* translated by David Magarshack (Harmondsworth, 1971), 300.
16. Graham Greene, *Monsignor Quixote* (Harmondsworth, 1983), 76-7
17. John 19:38.
18. R. S. Thomas, 'Sure' in *Mass for Hard Times* (Newcastle, 1992), 53.
19. John 20:28.

CHAPTER 10: HEAVENLY BESTIARY: THE FOUR LIVING CREATURES
1. Bruno Bettelheim, *The Uses of Enchantment* (London, 1978).

2. *CT* 23-24, 28.
3. *CT*, 52.
4. *CT*, 54.
5. Romans 7:24.
6. Janet Malcolm, *Psychoanalysis: The Impossible Profession* (New York, 1982), 119. I am indebted to Alan Jones, *Soul Making* (London, 1986) for introducing me to this perceptive book.
7. Nikolaus Pevsner, *The Buildings of England: Worcestershire* (Harmondsworth, 1968), 307.
8. Revelation 4:6-8.
9. Matthew 28:20.
10. Julian of Norwich, *Revelations of Divine Love*, chapter 27; ibid, 57.
11. Mark 1:12,13.

CHAPTER 11: WHO IS LIKE GOD? ST MICHAEL AND SATAN

1. Exodus 3:6, 6:3.
2. Isaiah 43:1.
3. Revelation 12:7-9.
4. Daniel 10:21.
5. Wilfred Owen, 'Soldier's Dream' in *Collected Poems*, edited by C. Day Lewis (London, 1963), 84.
6. 'Death, be not proud', the tenth of the 'Holy Sonnets'; *The Poems of John Donne*, Edited by Herbert J. C. Grierson (Oxford, 1951), I, 326.
7. John 19:30.
8. C. S. Lewis, *The Great Divorce* (London, 1977), 112-113.
9. Hosea 2:14,15.
10. George Herbert, 'The Temper' in *Works*, 102.

CHAPTER 12: CUP OF BLESSING: THE CHALICE AND THE SERPENT

1. CT, 37.
2. Revelation 12:11.
3. Hosea 11:4. The imagery here is often said to be of the loving *father* caring for his child. I find it more natural to read the metaphor as a *maternal* one.
4. *The Quest of the Holy Grail*, translated by P.M. Matarasso (Harmondsworth, 1969), 43,44.
5. See chapter 2, note 6.
6. Romans 8:21.
7. *Alternative Service Book 1980*, 512. This collect for the Third Sunday of Lent was borrowed from the Episcopal Church of the USA.
8. George Herbert, 'The Agony' in *The Temple* (Works, London, n.d.) 82.
9. Amy Carmichael, cited Alan Jones, *Passion for Pilgrimage* (San Francisco, 1989), 136.
10. 1 Corinthians 15:22.
11. See Tissa Balasuriya, *The Eucharist and Human Liberation* (London, 1979).
12. John 3:14,15.
13. 1 Corinthians 11:26.
14. John 21:15-19.

CHAPTER 13: WHOLLY WITHIN LOVE: THE HUMAN FIGURE

1. Percy Bysshe Shelley, 'Ozymandias' in *Complete Poetical Works* (London, 1907), 546.
2. Job 38:3.
3. Luke 9:34.
4. Genesis 32:22-31.
5. Alan Ecclestone, *The Night Sky of the Lord* (London, 1980).

6. *The Cloud of Unknowing*, chapter 14, edited by Justin McCann (London, 1943), 24
7. F. Dostoevsky, *The Brothers Karamazov*, 298.
8. Rudolph Otto, *The Idea of the Holy* (London, 1925).
9. *The Cloud of Unknowing*, Chapter 6.
10. R. S. Thomas, 'Pilgrimages' in *Later Poems 1972-1982* (London, 1984), 125.
11. Madeleine L'Engle, *Lines Scribbled on an Envelope* (New York, 1969), 49; cited Alan Jones, *Soul Making*, 49.
12. T. S. Eliot, 'East Coker' in *Four Quartets, Collected Poems 1909-1962*, 200.

CHAPTER 14: THE WOMB OF THE WORLD: THE MANDORLA

1. Robert Browning, 'Bishop Blougram's Apology' in *Poetical Works* (London, n.d.), 640.
2. 'The Second Coming' in A. N. Jeffares, ed., *W. B. Yeats: Selected Poetry* (London, 1967), 99.
3. Wilfrid Gibson, 'Lament' in *Oxford Book of Twentieth Century Verse*, 144.
4. The conclusion of the prayer traditionally ascribed to St Francis of Assisi.
5. John Donne, *Death's Duel* (his last sermon) in Logan Pearsall Smith, ed., *Donne's Sermons* (Oxford, 1919), 238.
6. T. S. Eliot, 'The Journey of the Magi' in *Collected Poems 1909-1962*, (London, 1974) 109.
7. John 3:3.
8. Romans 6:11.

CHAPTER 15: AT THE CENTRE: 'BEHOLD A MAN'

1. *The Complete Poems*, 506
2. 1 Corinthians 13:8.
3. T. S. Eliot, 'East Coker' in *Four Quartets, Collected Poems 1909-1962*, 196.
4. Proverbs 27:6 (AV).
5. Luke 22:60-62.
6. 2 Samuel 12:7 (AV).
7. John 21:27.
8. John 20:15-16.
9. John 20:25, 28.
10. 'The face of Christ is going to be your greatest work, and I am sure you will succeed. Victory, serenity, compassion will be a great challenge to combine. Just as the Italians boldly conceived an Italian face for Christ, and the Spanish a Spanish face, it may come to you to conceive an English face, universal at the same time.' So Provost Howard to Graham Sutherland in 1953, *CT* 24.
11. 1 John 3:2.
12. Romans 8:21, 29; Ephesians 4:13.
13. Luke 15:11-32.
14. Pace Daphne Hampson in an article entitled 'God, Gender and Human Equality', in *The Independent*, 13 November 1993, in which the tapestry is seen as expressing and reinforcing Christianity's preoccupation with masculine images. What provoked the observation was the irony, as she saw it, of a service arranged by the Movement for the Ordination of Women having taken place in front of the tapestry.
15. This now famous phrase was first used by D. W. Winnicott in his paper 'Ego distortion in terms of true and false self' in *The Maturational Processes and the Facilitating Environment* (New York,), 145.
16. Ephesians 4:10.
17. Hebrews 1:3.
18. John 19:5.
19. *CT*, 29-31.
20. Hebrew 2:9.
21. Hebrews 2:18.

22. Alice Meynell, 'Christ in the Universe' in *Poems* (London, 1921), 114.
23. Paul Davies, *The Mind of God* (New York, 1992), 194ff.
24. Augustine of Hippo, *The City of God*, translated by John Healey (London, 1945), II, 408.

CHAPTER 16: THE SIGNATURE

1. Peter Matthieson, *The Snow Leopard*, 271.
2. *The Mathnawi*, a 13th century poem by Maulana Jalalu'ddin Rumi, translated by R. A. Nicholson (London, 1934), quoted in Betsy Caprio & Thomas M. Hedberg, *Coming Home* (Mahwah, New Jersey, 1986), 75.
3. Julian Green, *Diary 1928-1957* (London, 1964), 119.
4. Anthony de Mello, *The Song of the Bird* (New York, 1984), 16.
5. Romans 12:1,2.
6. Dietrich Bonhoeffer, *Letters and Papers from Prison* (London, 1959), 121-122.
7. 1 Corinthians 16:21.
8. Galatians 6:11.
9. Viktor E. Frankl, *Man's Search for Meaning: an introduction to logotherapy,* translated by Ilse Lasch (London, 1962), 117.
10. Deuteronomy 6:4,5.
11. Thornton Wilder, *The Bridge of San Luis Rey* (London, 1928), 140.

ACKNOWLEDGEMENTS

The publishers wish to express their gratitude to the following for permission to reproduce copyright material:

Chatto & Windus, 20 Vauxhall Bridge Road, London SW1V 2SA for the extract from *The Snow Leopard* by Peter Matthieson.

J. M. Dent & Sons Ltd, Orion House, 5 Upper St Martin's Lane, London WC2H 9EA for the extract from 'Poetry for Supper' from *Collected Poems 1945-1990* by R. S. Thomas.

Faber & Faber Ltd, 3 Queen Square, London WC1N 3AU for extracts from 'Little Gidding', 'The Journey of the Magi' and 'East Coker', taken from *Collected Poems 1909-1962* by T. S. Eliot; extract from 'Days', taken from *The Whitsun Weddings* by Philip Larkin, and extract from *High Windows* by Philip Larkin.

David Higham Associates, 5-8 Lower John Street, Golden Square, London W1R 4HA for the extract from 'The Shaking World' by Elizabeth Jennings from *Collected Poems*, published by Carcanet. Also, the extract from *Monsignor Quixote* by Graham Greene, published by The Bodley Head.

MacMillan London Ltd, Cavaye Place, London SW10 9PG for the extract from *Pilgrimages* by R. S. Thomas.

Penguin Books Ltd, Bath Road, Harmondsworth, West Drayton, Middlesex UB7 ODA for the short quotation from *The Brothers Karamazov* by F. Dostoevsky, translated by David Magarshack (Penguin Classics 1958) (page 300), © copyright David Magarshack 1958. Also, the extract from *The Quest of the Holy Grail*, translated by P. M. Matarasso, (Penguin Classics, 1969) (pp 43-44) © copyright P. M. Matarasso, 1969.